Praise for

CREATING SIGNATURE STORIES

"A great story for storytellers everywhere. David Aaker's in-depth look at what makes a great story plus his powerful examples are a shining example for brands, marketers and all of us who recognize the power of signature stories to inspire, motivate, sell and drive our companies forward."

Linda Boff, VP & CMO, GE

"The father of modern branding, David Aaker argues persuasively that in our hyper-growing but fragmented digital, social and content worlds, effective brand storytelling cuts through the noise, and skepticism to connect with the hearts and minds of today's employees, consumers, and customers."

Cheryl Burgess, CEO, Blue Focus Marketing and
author of *"The Social Employee"*

"Aaker, the branding guru, demonstrates how to find or create signature stories that are intriguing, authentic, and engaging and how to manage them to energize your brand to persuade and inspire to action employees and customers."

Peter Guber, Chairman and CEO of Mandalay Entertainment,
author of *"Tell to Win"*

"The reason Dave Aaker's books are so good is that he invariably breaks new ground—both in terms of what you didn't know, as well as what you thought you knew, but maybe didn't really. Brand stories and story-telling have become quite fashionable in marketing circles, although often without much depth. Once again, Dave skillfully builds a rich, practical framework that is as original as it is relevant. His blueprint for creating signature stories is one that needs to be carefully studied and applied."

Kevin Lane Keller, E.B. Osborn Professor of Marketing, Tuck School of Business

"Every brand carries many stories. Some stories are interesting but soon forgotten. David Aaker defines the signature story that gets deep into the consumers' consciousness. The company's job is to find and guide its signature stories."

Philip Kotler, S.C. Johnson & Son Distinguished Professor of International Marketing, Kellogg School of Management, Northwestern University

"Dr. Aaker, the founding father of branding, has provided books and insights indispensable to our efforts to build the branding discipline in Korea over 20 years. He has done it again with another pioneering book. *Creating Signature Stories* will bring more clarity, more direction, and more life for brands struggling to inspire employees and break through marketplace clutter."

Jerry Lee and Katy Choi, Partners, Brand and Company

"David Aaker's *Creating Signature Stories* reminds us that in a mad world where marketing messages bombard you 24/7 across every channel, going back to basics is the winning strategy. Great story-telling and the power of word-of-mouth (now possible at scale through social media) have never been more important. Intriguing, authentic, empathic brand stories, not just features and facts, are what people gravitate toward and remember."

Ann Lewnes, Executive Vice President & CMO, Adobe

"I first heard the material in this book at an event where I both introduced Dave Aaker and closed the event. As I listened I thought: Hey, what if I close with a crack at my own signature story? The audience was just right—mostly alums of the school where I'm dean. I went for it, offering details on what makes me that I've never discussed publicly, including points about my family and defining experiences from my past. I did my best to deliver emotional impact and a sense for why it all matters. Many people approached me afterward and told me it worked. And thanked me. Now it's my turn to thank Dave. (And yes, I felt the best endorsement for this book would be story.)"

Rich Lyons, Dean Berkeley Haas School of Business

"If you ever wanted to know the science behind successful story telling in marketing, *CREATING SIGNATURE STORIES* is the book! David Aaker is not only a great story teller, he is also a great scientist"

Jagdish N. Sheth, Charles Kellstadt Professor of
Marketing Emory University

"Marketers obsessed with the data and analytics are missing the true 'secret formula' of connecting with people: memorable, signature storytelling. Professor Aaker has brilliantly distilled the critical elements of signature storytelling to give us a roadmap for higher levels of personal engagement."

Joe Tripodi, CMO Subway and former CMO of Coca-Cola, Allstate, and MasterCard

"Today, we see many leading brands focus on building strong relationship with consumers with compelling stories, presented and amplified in the right way. This brilliant book helps brands structure and create signature content to engage consumers effectively. We at Alibaba, the primary brand marketing ecosystem, also aim to help brands create and deliver stories in various intriguing and innovative ways via the digital experience."

Chris Tung, CMO, Alibaba Group

Also by David Aaker

Aaker on Branding: 20 Principles that Drive Success

Brand Relevance: Making Competitors Irrelevant

Three Threats to Brand Relevance (e-book)

Spanning Silos: The New CMO Imperative

Building Strong Brands

Brand Leadership (with Erich Joachimsthaler)

From Fargo to the World of Brands: My Story So Far

*Brand Portfolio Strategy: Creating Relevance,
Differentiation, Energy, Leverage, and Clarity*

Managing Brand Equity

*Strategic Market Management (11ᵗʰ edition)
(with Christine Moorman)*

Brand Equity and Advertising (edited with Alexander Biel)

*Marketing Research 11 Edition
(with V. Kumar, Robert Leone, and George Day)*

Advertising Management 5th Edition
(with Rajeev Batra and John Myers)

Multivariate Analysis in Marketing (2nd edition)

Consumerism: Search for the Consumer Interest
(edited with Georgy Day)

CREATING SIGNATURE STORIES

CREATING SIGNATURE STORIES

STRATEGIC MESSAGING
THAT PERSUADES, ENERGIZES
AND INSPIRES

DAVID AAKER

NEW YORK

LONDON • NASHVILLE • MELBOURNE • VANCOUVER

Creating Signature Stories

Strategic Messaging that Energizes, Persuades and Inspires

Published in New York, New York, by Morgan James Publishing. Morgan James is a trademark of Morgan James, LLC. www.MorganJamesPublishing.com

The Morgan James Speakers Group can bring authors to your live event. For more information or to book an event visit The Morgan James Speakers Group at www.TheMorganJamesSpeakersGroup.com.

ISBN 9781683506119 paperback
ISBN 9781683506126 eBook
Library of Congress Control Number: 2017908870

Interior Design by:
Chris Treccani
www.3dogcreative.net

To my wife Kay and
my daughters Jennifer, Jan, and Jolyn and their families.
They all support and inspire me every day.

Table of Contents

Acknowledgments

This book was stimulated by the work of my daughter Jennifer Aaker on the vast power of stories. Jennifer, a professor at the Stanford Graduate School of Business, is a pioneering researcher, a gifted and innovative teacher, a giving person and an incredible daughter. She got me into pursuing the strength of stories, and it was our vigorous discussions that helped me create and refine the core ideas. It was a joy to spend time with her, trying out theories and material.

I owe much gratitude to those many authors—including Annette Simmons, Peter Guber, Stephen Denning and Jack Maguire—who have explored storytelling in all its forms and made its practice available to a wide audience. And to the researchers in psychology and management who have shown so vividly with experiments and theory the power of stories to gain visibility and energy, to persuade and to inspire. And to those in organizations who have used stories so effectively and thus demonstrated their power in challenging contexts.

Many of my ideas—and the book title itself—have come from or been nurtured by my colleagues at Prophet, the global brand and strategy consulting firm with which I have been associated since 1999. I thank CEO Michael Dunn for his support and friendship, as well as Scott Davis, Andy Pierce and Rune Gustafson for their inspiration. Paul Wang and the San Francisco design team all contributed cover ideas.

The marketing team of John Baglivo, Amanda Nizzere, Lindsay Malone and Amy Bennett along with Ariel Grazer and Jonathan Redman helped with the marketing strategy and made sure that the book got exposure inside and outside Prophet.

I have been delighted with my partners at Morgan James Publishing, who replace stress in the process with confidence, creativity and fun. David Hancock, its founder and CEO, is knowledgeable, insightful and supportive, and has been such a pleasure to work with. Jim Howard, its publisher, added helpful advice at crucial times. My brilliant copy editor, Dan Cooreman, elevated the book for sure and in the process taught me tons about writing and wordsmithing.

Finally, I would like to thank my family—my wife, Kay, and our daughters, Jennifer, Jan, and Jolyn, as well as their families—who continuously support and inspire me, and enrich my life.

WHAT IS A SIGNATURE STORY?

"A story is a way to say something that can't be said
any other way"
—Flannery O'Connor, American storyteller

A Founder Story

Leon L. Bean, an avid outdoorsman, returned from a hunting trip in 1912 disgruntled because of his cold, wet feet. With few resources but a lot of motivation and ingenuity, he invented a new boot by stitching lightweight leather tops to waterproof rubber bottoms. The boots worked so well that he offered them for sale via mail order as the Maine Hunting Shoe, using lists of nonresident holders of Maine hunting licenses. Unfortunately, 90 of the first 100 pairs sold had a stitching problem and leaked.

Leon Bean faced a defining moment! His response? He refunded the customers' money even though it nearly broke him, and he fixed the process so that future boots were indeed water-tight. The **L.L. Bean** story shows a firm that has an innovation culture, a heritage around fishing and hunting (which has since been generalized to the outdoors), a commitment to quality and a concern for customers reflected in its legendary guarantee of "100 percent satisfaction."

An Offering Story

Natalia, a 15-year-old girl in a small village in Mozambique, had a life that revolved around water. Each morning, after caring for her six siblings, she would walk with pails to a riverbed and stand in line waiting to get dirty water from a hand-dug hole, a task that took hours. That meant she could go to school only twice each week. But in 2012, thanks to **charity: water**, a nonprofit group that brings clean, safe drinking water to people in developing countries, her village received a well, allowing residents to pump as much clean water as they needed, easily and quickly. Natalia was now always at school and on time. No exceptions.

The village's five-person water committee was tasked with developing and implementing a business plan to ensure the project's long-term sustainability and with educating the community about health, sanitation and hygiene. When charity: water met with the committee, the last member stood to introduce herself—her feet wide apart, her arms crossed proudly, and with a pleased half-smile on her face: "My name is Natalia," she said. "I am the president." By far the youngest in such a position, Natalia was selected because of her confidence, tenacity, leadership skills and the fact that she could read and write. Her ambition has changed. She now plans to become a teacher and then a headmaster. Her story puts a personal touch on the efforts of charity: water, whose nearly 23,000 projects in its first eight years have made clean water available to over seven million people.

A Brand Story

To celebrate people who would do "Anything for Hockey," the brewer **Molson Canadian** decided to create a professionally-made hockey rink high in the Purcell Mountains in British Columbia. Not at all easy—building a rink in such a remote spot and then selecting players for an event there! It took two weeks and many helicopter trips to construct the rink, complete with an iconic Molson refrigerator. Players were selected based on their personal stories about their obsession with hockey. Eleven winners and the actual Stanley Cup (the ultimate hockey symbol) were flown in for a game at this unique space. For those passionate about hockey, the event brought shivers of excitement.

The global story detailed the program's execution: finding the site, building the rink using the helicopter, choosing the winners and staging the game itself. The story shows vividly how Molson shared its customers' passion for hockey by creating a program with "Can you believe it?" uniqueness and emotional impact. The story, which injects energy and the tactile feel of cold and ice into the brand, can be contrasted to those of other beers that focus only on the product's pleasures.

A Customer Story

IBM Watson Health applies to health care the power of IBM's Watson, a software platform that lets a firm manage a huge amount of stored information and data. Orlando Health, a private, not-for-profit network, had seemingly intractable problems inhibiting efforts to contain costs and deliver patient care. What to do? The solution: Leverage Watson technology to enable a new health management system.

The story details the problems of the prior system, the goals of the new system, the implemented changes and various achievement measures.[1] The results? Updated and streamlined processes and a transition from "fee for service" reimbursement to payment models that reward coordinated total care, including preventive care tailored to the individual. It brought more than 10 percent improvement in first-year measures like the share of people over 50 who received a colonoscopy, the share of adult women who received preventive mammogram screening, and the share of patients who received depression screening.

This story is exceptionally relevant to other health care networks with similar challenges and aspirations. The story offers heart and clarity not only for the IBM Watson Health brand but also for the IBM Watson brand and even the IBM brand itself, because everyone can appreciate solutions that lead to better health care at reduced cost.

A Growth Strategy Story

On August 2, 2006, two years before the first **Tesla** car was shipped, Elon Musk presented his growth story for the company even though he was a part-timer—his day job was to run another business, SpaceX. The core challenge was how a new electric car company could get a foothold in an auto industry with such long-established firms. His four-step growth story provides not only the answer, but also credibility and inspiration to employees, customers and investors—all groups that need to see substance as well as goals.

Musk's memo was titled "The Secret Tesla Motors Master Plan (just between you and me)." Step 1: Build a high-end electric sports car (the Tesla Roadster) that performs better than existing gas-powered cars like the Porsche and has twice the energy efficiency of a Prius, then use the proceeds to help fund the next stage. Step 2: Build a more affordable four-door, luxury sedan (the Model S) and again use the proceeds to help fund the next stage. Step 3: Build an even more affordable sedan (the Model 3) that generates high-volume economies of scale. Step 4: During this process, provide zero-emission, electric power generation options using modestly sized and priced solar panels from Musk's SolarCity that can be employed to recharge the Tesla batteries. News items about Tesla's journey became part of the growth story.

The plan played out, and in July 2016 Musk added four new elements: Create solar roofs for homes integrated with battery storage. Build cars for all major market segments. Develop a self-driving capability 10 times safer than human drivers. And enable cars to be rented to others when not in use. It seemed risky to bet against Musk.

A Borrowed Story

In the early 1990s, Peter Guber became CEO of **Columbia Pictures Entertainment**, which had just been acquired by Sony. He tells of how he needed to re-energize Columbia, which in addition to its moviemaking business included global television operations and the Loews theaters.[2] He describes a firm that had been in disarray with revenue in free fall, discouraged employees and a bunch of disparate units lacking a unified vision and spread out over the country—and now it had a foreign owner. There was a need to reframe the situation, and the story of Lawrence of Arabia did just that.

T.E. Lawrence, a British military officer in World War I known for ignoring established norms, was advising Prince Faisal in his revolt against the Ottomans. After a major defeat, Lawrence's British superiors advised a retreat. Instead, Lawrence proposed a daring attack on Aqaba, a strategic Ottoman port that was protected inland by what seemed to be an impassible desert. The plan was to have a small band of fighters cross that desert—with its intense heat, snakes, scorpions and lack of water—and surprise the Ottoman garrison. Gaining the support of Prince Faisal and of some very independent Bedouin desert tribes more accustomed to fighting one another than cooperating, Lawrence and the fighters accomplished the impossible and took Aqaba. The story of their success, told and retold around the world, provided a way forward in a messy war. And, of course, Columbia's award-winning film "Lawrence of Arabia," starring Peter O'Toole, would later record the victory with all its suspense, emotion and detail.

In this tale of an unlikely alliance of Arab tribes working together with an outsider to overcome enormous odds, Guber found a signature story. He offered that Columbia could also pull together under its new owner—by uniting a disparate group of businesses into a single force—and make the impossible possible. He started by telling the story during an annual Christmas event at the company and presented executives with framed copies of a photograph of a robed O'Toole. The story clicked, and "Aqaba" became a rallying cry. It changed the mind-set of the organization, led to a revitalized employee base, created a unified organization directed from a single location, supported an innovative growth strategy and prompted a name change to Sony Pictures Entertainment. Many years later, those pictures of O'Toole are still in the offices.

Using Stories to Communicate Strategic Messaging

This book shows how to apply the power of storytelling to strategic messaging in the age of social media. And it explains why storytelling is so helpful—and often necessary—in making your message come alive. It is based on three observations:

First, **stories are powerful.** The potential power of storytelling in management, often underappreciated, came to me from the work of my daughter Jennifer, a professor at the Stanford Graduate School of Business. Jennifer has attracted much attention over the last seven years for her research, teaching and speaking about the topic. She has pointed me to extensive research in psychology and elsewhere that shows how stories are orders of magnitude more powerful than sets of facts, no matter how those facts are packaged. Orders of magnitude! Stories are superior to facts in gaining exposure, activating social media, communicating information, being remembered, creating involvement, persuading, inspiring and more. Way superior.

Consider the examples in this chapter. Listing just the simple facts about the Maine Hunting Shoe, the Mozambique village's water supply, the Molson mountain hockey rink, the power of IBM's Watson, the growth plans of Tesla or the achievements of Lawrence of Arabia would gain much less attention and have far less impact than their compelling stories.

If you have facts to communicate, your best strategy is to find or create a story that allows the ultimate message to emerge, or at least motivates the facts so they are more likely to be heard. Find a way to turn the facts into a story, perhaps by telling how a program started, how a new process yielded a superior product, or how a customer used that product to accomplish a difficult goal. Or find a story that can otherwise put the facts into an interesting and relevant context.

Second, **content is king in the digital age, and stories are the key to content.** The social-media audience isn't passive; it is in control. It involves itself in messaging only when it is intrigued by content. Thus, content drives success in this new era—and content, in turn, is all about stories.

Facts, no matter how compelling, rarely gain the attention or processing necessary to emerge from a crowded media landscape. Stories provide a way to break through all the distractions, disinterest and content overload and make an audience take notice. People perk up when they hear someone say, "Let me tell you a story." Because a story is much more likely to be involving than a set of facts, it can also keep people's attention and linger in their memory.

Partly because organizations feel pressure to be relevant in the digital era, stories have become a hot topic in marketing communication. Many firms have added processes and structures that enable them to find, create and evaluate strong stories. They have also added journalists and filmmakers to their staffs to present these stories in a compelling way. The agency world now includes communication firms staffed by former top journalists who help organizations and their leaders with these tasks. [3]

Third, **communicating a strategic message is extremely difficult**, especially amid the media clutter of the digital world. In my work on brands and branding, I have seen at first hand the tough challenge of showing what a brand stands for—whether the audience is inside or outside the organization. The same can be said for communicating organizational values or other strategic messaging.

Why is the task so hard? Your customers and employees are often not that interested in your strategic message, or even in your organization, brands, products or services. The story's role is to provide that missing interest. Customers and employees may also view your strategic message as lacking authenticity and credibility. An effective story reduces this risk because the story's heroes and plot become the focus, and counter-arguing becomes much less likely.

Tactical vs. strategic messaging. In this book, the focus is not just stories, but signature stories, those that communicate a strategic message that is relevant to the brand vision, the customer relationship, the organization and its values and/or the business strategy. The six stories starting this chapter are signature stories and are strategic assets to their brand and firm.

A signature story can be contrasted with a tactical story. There is a qualitative difference, so the two must be resourced and managed very differently.

A tactical story is used to achieve a short-term communication objective, perhaps in an advertisement or on a website. There is no expectation that the story will live beyond its communication task.

A signature story has a message, role and life that are very different. Charged with communicating a strategic message, the signature story will be an enduring, relevant asset that can provide continuing direction. As the story is retold and reappears, it will gain authenticity, traction and influence. Ultimately, some signature stories will be meaningful enough to fuel growth in success measures like sales, profits and market position.

The barriers to story use. Given the power of stories and the importance of content, why aren't stories used more extensively to communicate strategic messaging? Three reasons stand out:

- Many people think that communicating facts with clarity and punch is more efficient than telling a story, with its indirect and partial message. When communicating four points is the goal, there may be no currently available story that works for all four—or even for two or three.
- Organizations, particularly in the business-to-business (b-to-b) and high-tech spheres, may assume that their audiences are always rational, motivated and able to find and process objective information. (This comfortable assumption, of course, rarely holds.)
- It is difficult to find and leverage great signature stories—those that attract attention, create interest and cause their audience to digest the content.

Despite the challenges and flawed assumptions, organizations must develop the ability to find or create stories that communicate strategic content. It's not enough to say you want to find a story that will package at least some of the important facts to be communicated. You must find the right story (or the right set of stories) and deliver a plan to give it exposure.

Defining Signature Stories

A story is here defined as a narrative that portrays actual or fictitious events or experiences with a beginning, a middle and an end (not always portrayed in that order). In doing so, the story provides an organizing framework for its components and implications. The story often has explicit or implied emotional content and detailed sensory information.

Importantly, a story is not a description of a set of facts (or features). It may incorporate and communicate facts, but in the context of a narrative—so the audience may need to deduce those facts. The story, however, can influence the interpretation of the facts and issues raised.

What is a **signature story**? It is an intriguing, authentic, involving narrative that delivers or supports a strategic message clarifying or enhancing the brand vision, customer relationship, organizational values and/or business strategy. It provides visibility and energy to brands and persuades and/or inspires employees and/or customers over an extended time.

A signature story needs to grab attention—to be **intriguing** if not fascinating. Without attention, nothing matters. Exposure to the story is not enough, because only small percentages of exposures are noticed and even fewer are processed. The story should attract the eye and the mind, offering some combination of thought-provoking, novel, informative, inspiring, exceptionally relevant, humorous or awe-creating content. Think of a story that has stuck in your memory. It will almost surely be extremely high in one or more of these seven characteristics.

One measure of "intriguing" is whether a story stimulates word-of-mouth communication personally and/or via social media. A case in point is an old story from Nordstrom that brings to life the empowerment of its salespeople. In one version of the story, a customer in the mid-1970s walked into its Fairbanks, Alaska, clothing store and asked to "return" two worn snow tires. An awkward moment! Nordstrom, of course, did not sell tires (although the store site was once a tire store). But the salesperson, who had been on the job only a few weeks, had no doubt about what to do. He promptly took back the tires and refunded what the customer said he had paid. I have asked many California audiences whether they have heard of the Nordstrom story, and usually one-third to one-half have raised hands. In nearly every case, people heard it not from Nordstrom but from other customers who found the story so novel and so representative of what Nordstrom stands for that they repeated it.

Authenticity means that the audience does not perceive the story to be phony, contrived or a transparent selling effort. Natalia's story provides the authenticity that comes from getting to know and admire a real person in a real setting.

A signature story, however, does not have to be real to be authentic. For example, an AT&T story about a realistic car accident caused by distracted driving is powerful even though it is clearly fictional; it has verisimilitude—the appearance of truth.

Authenticity also means that there is substance behind the story and its strategic message in the form of transparency, policies and programs. Without supporting substance to confirm and solidify the message, a story's authenticity is undercut and the brand is ultimately tarnished. All six stories in this chapter offer much supporting substance:

- L.L. Bean delivers its quality promise and guarantee and shows its passion for the outdoors in many ways, including its L.L. Bean Outdoor Discovery Schools where fly-fishing, kayaking and outdoor photography are only a few of the dozens of adventures on tap.
- The charity: water organization obtains clean water for villages that are without.
- Molson has supported its "Anything for Hockey" story in several ways, including an ongoing sponsorship of the N.H.L., an offer to fans to watch games at a Molson Canadian Hockey House and the construction of a rink atop a 32-story building in downtown Toronto.
- IBM Watson Health improves the effectiveness and efficiency of medical care.

- Tesla raises capital and implements its plan.
- Lawrence of Arabia successfully took Aqaba, and Columbia brought its organizational units together to perform much better than some had predicted possible.

Involving means that the audience is drawn into the story. You empathize with the characters. The plot becomes important. The result is usually, but not always, a cognitive, emotional and/or behavioral response.

Cognitively, the audience processes the story and its theme and accepts its major points. In the charity: water story, the audience can understand the risks and time costs of the village's old system and appreciate the organization's efforts to solve the problem of tainted water. A cognitive response is also important for most b-to-b contexts in which a successful customer application is detailed—as in the story of IBM Watson Health. There, the driver of involvement is relevance. A signature story needs to reflect meaningful problems faced by its audience.

Emotionally, an involving story can precipitate feelings about the characters but sometimes also about its surprise or climax. There was nostalgia created by the vision of Leon Bean duck hunting, a feeling of pride in the charity: water story for Natalia's achievements and future, exhilaration for those who played on Molson's mountain hockey rink, satisfaction in seeing IBM Watson Health resolve a difficult problem, and amazement at Tesla's risk-taking and Lawrence's courage.

Behaviorally, a story can motivate audience members to take action when the time is right. They might tell friends or colleagues the Molson or IBM Watson Health stories or consider Tesla when buying a car. Or they might see L.L. Bean or Nordstrom as a shopping destination. Or they might donate to charity: water. Or organizational units at Columbia might be inspired to work together toward an audacious goal.

A signature story will have a **strategic message** that is relevant to its audience and clarifies or enhances the following, both internally and externally:

- **The brand vision.** All six stories clarify or enhance a brand's visibility, image, personality, relevance and/or value proposition.
- **The customer relationship.** The "Anything for Hockey" program supports and adds emotion to Molson's shared interest in hockey with its customers. Natalia's story shows the relationship between charity: water and its clients.
- **The organization and its values.** The IBM Watson Health story reflects the organizational commitment to changing health care by leveraging the power of IBM Watson. The Tesla story validates its mission to move the country closer to sustainability.
- **The present and future business strategy.** All six stories represent the core of a present or future business strategy. A frequent challenge, especially within an organization, is to communicate a new business strategy and the changes that must accompany it. A signature story can usually do the job much better than facts or simple logical reasoning.

A signature story is a strategic asset that provides visibility and energy to the brand and persuades or inspires employees and/or customers over an extended time. These six stories accomplish all these tasks. The Molson story, for example, creates brand visibility and energy by involving the audience in an activity they care about. It persuades by reinforcing the perception that Molson is serious about hockey and those who share its passion. Finally, it inspires—because the emotion surrounding its rink-building feat will linger and be attached to the Molson brand.

A word of caution: The degree to which a signature story meets its four criteria—to be intriguing, authentic and involving, and to have a strategic message—must be judged by those who develop and use it. But they should resist the temptation to elevate to signature status a story that is weak in one or more of these four dimensions.

A Signature Story Is Not a Set of Facts

A signature story is a narrative, a "once upon a time ..." narrative. It is not a set of facts or a list of features. For me, this was the conceptual breakthrough that enabled this book to go forward. It came after many patient discussions (well, O.K., not always patient) over several years with my daughter Jennifer, the Stanford professor, who has done extensive teaching and research on storytelling.

The core problem is that some people describe almost any kind of communication as a "story." When they do so, however, the concept of a story has no consistently useful meaning.

Consider the way firms are encouraged to develop a "company story" or a "brand story." By that, they mean to address questions like these:

- Describe your organization. What does you company do?
- What are its values? Its strategy?
- Who are your customer targets?
- What is your value proposition for each segment?
- What is your point of difference?

Answers to such questions often involve lists of facts. These lists should certainly be perused, as they provide a solid underpinning for a strategy and a brand vision—often crucial to success. But the result is not a story as here defined.

As noted at the outset of the chapter, presenting a set of facts about an organization or brand seems appealing because it appears to communicate a lot of information efficiently and completely. By contrast, a signature story might communicate only a small part of the "list" and perhaps only indirectly. The charity: water signature story about Natalia impacts but communicates only a few of the facts about the program on the organization's list of communication objectives. The IBM Watson Health story about Orlando Health is specific, and comparable organizations can relate to it, but it provides only a limited perspective of IBM Watson Health's role in improving health care.

A set of facts, though often attractive to those facing a communication task, is not a signature story—an authentic narrative that intrigues, involves and carries a strategic message. In fact, such a fact set is often perceived as boring rather than intriguing, as conveying puffery instead of authenticity, and as too similar to comparable lists from other organizations to be involving. A signature story, by contrast, will be more likely to gain attention, persuade and inspire.

What should be done in an important strategic communication when descriptive facts capture so well what the brand, organization or strategy is about? First, recognize that a set of facts can guide and inspire *only* if it is heard and gains buy-in—but that is rarely the case. Second, explore how stories can accomplish or help to accomplish the same objective. Sometimes, a set of facts can be turned into a story by providing a context and more information. Recall how E.M. Forster explained what a story is: If you are told that the king died and then the queen died, that is a sequence of events. If you are told that the king died and that the queen then died of grief, that is a story.

Signature Stories Need Not Replace Facts

By themselves, facts may not do well at gaining attention, persuading, inspiring, etc. But they can seal the deal. They can provide substance that will make the case more convincing and thus more resistant to future counter-communication. They can also add clarity to the story's point. Presenting facts in the context of the story—and not by themselves—can thus be helpful. There are three ways to do that.

Embed facts into the story. When feasible, the best option is to introduce facts in the flow of the narrative. Rather than looking like an "add-on," they should add credibility or detail to an aspect of the story, perhaps to make the challenge more vivid or credible, provide motivation for a character or add detail to a scene, in a way that fits rather than detracts.

Sometimes, however, facts just do not fit well into the story, so alternatives are needed.

Place facts after the story. In this option, the story gains the audience's attention, entices involvement into the context, distracts from counter-arguing and provides a reason to process the facts that follow it. The story should provide a basis for believing the facts and for understanding that facts are needed to bring the story to completion. In the charity: water example, the story sets up the facts of the program—how many wells and how people are affected. After the Nordstrom story is told, the presenter might describe the chain's policy of empowerment—how salespeople have access to the entire store to satisfy a shopper's interest and have authority to make many decisions. The story makes these facts more relevant and interesting.

Andy Rubin, co-founder of Android, introduced his new company, Essential Products, with a story.[4] It all started, he said, during a night out with an old friend: "As the night went on we inevitably began talking about what we didn't like about the current state of technology. Less and less choice. More and more unnecessary features cluttering our lives. An increasing sea of products that didn't work with one another." After another long talk, he said, "we decided that I needed to start a new kind of company using 21st-century methods to build products for the way people want to live in the 21st century." It was only after this story that Rubin set forth the new company's six bullet-point principles, such as "simple is always better." Without the story motivating and positioning the principles of the new company, few would process and digest them.

The trick is to introduce the fact presentation so that it adds to or completes the story and does not diminish the story's authenticity by turning it into a selling experience or an exercise in puffery. If the story is compelling and told well, and if the fact presentation is relevant and compact, this risk is reduced.

Place facts before the story. In this final option, the facts are presented first, and the story's role is to add motivation and credibility to them—and bring them to life with richness and vividness. One firm might use a story to provide a "wow!" factor after a fact description. The story should also soften the tendency to counter-argue, and should elevate the fact-teller's credibility. In the case of Nordstrom, the facts could come before the story instead of after. The audience would first be told the facts about the policy of employee involvement and then be told the "let me illustrate what I am talking about" story.

A facts-first strategy works when the facts themselves are punchy and at least somewhat intriguing—and are not drawn out. Molson has built a hockey rink high in a mountain range. I want to hear more. Facts shouldn't make anyone lose interest before getting to the story.

A danger of the facts-first option is that facts can create an analytical mind-set that undercuts the story's power. One study showed that if respondents were given an analytical exercise before hearing a story, they would respond similarly to a group that heard a set of facts instead of the story. This risk is reduced if the speaker is known and considered credible and "caring" at an emotional level.

A Signature Story Can Be Short

A signature story can be short on details; it does not have to be comprehensive. The audience can be expected to fill in some gaps. In fact, leaving some details to the imagination can be an effective way to involve the audience, letting it tailor the story to its experience. That was certainly the case for classic radio dramas like "The Shadow" and

"Dragnet," whose rapt audiences could picture and embellish many plot and character details in their minds.

A story can also be short in length. In fact, condensing stories to a few words can be a useful exercise. Literary legend has it that Ernest Hemingway once won a wager that he could write a six-word novel. His result, "For sale: baby shoes, never worn," was a work of which he was reportedly proud. The reader can fill in the details—about the death of a baby, the appearance and anguish of the mother as she sells the baby shoes, and perhaps the happiness of another mother who buys the shoes.

Even a metaphor can be a story, allowing its audience to visualize and embellish it. Consider these three metaphors about taxes: Taxes are a burden (see a person carrying a heavy backpack to a far-off tax collector). Taxes are paying your dues (see someone going to a country club to pay the annual fee to use its facilities). Taxes are investing in the future (see someone observing roads and bridges that will benefit future generations).

A Signature Story Can Be in the Minds of Customers, Employees or Others

A signature story can be unique to an individual. It may be influenced by a brand or organization, but the person forms and owns the story and its details. Although it exists only in his or her mind, such an ownable story can be more powerful and more likely to be retold than if it came from an organization.

Consider the Toyota Prius, which has dominated the hybrid market since it first appeared in the late 1990s. Around 3.5 million were sold worldwide in its first 15 years. The motivation of many of its users is the chance to express a commitment to the environment. A Prius owner's story might be some variation on the following:

> I am concerned about climate change and the environment; I think about it a lot. I want to do whatever I can to be part of the solution. When it came time to buy a car, I decided to buy a hybrid that would reduce gasoline consumption and thus carbon emissions. But which hybrid? After looking at several, I was attracted to the Prius because of its Toyota "Synergy Drive" technology and its pleasing and graceful design. (Here, my subconscious self is noting that when I drive a Prius, my friends and neighbors will know I am in a hybrid without me having to tell them.) The price was in my range, so everything fell into place and I pulled the trigger. Driving out of the showroom, I felt proud that I was matching my words and heart with tangible commitment. It was also nice to drop the fact that I bought a Prius into conversations with my golf buddies and my brother-in-law.

The story gains impact because it is owned by a customer, not by the brand or firm. But the firm can indirectly support the story by drawing attention to how a Prius reduces carbon emissions. Such efforts would normally be conventional product communication, but in the context of the story they play a different role.

A story that resides in the mind can be stimulated by the brand. For example, Burberry's "Art of the Trench" website encourages users to upload pictures of themselves wearing the iconic Burberry trench coat. Behind each picture, of course, is a meaningful personal story. The uploaded pictures can then be selected for the site, where they can be liked and shared by a huge global audience. The program, started in 2009, has been a part of Burberry's digital and e-commerce success. In the first year alone, the site had 7.5 million views from 150 countries. It supports the Burberry vision of being fashion-forward and a "democratic luxury" while creating a link to youthful, aspirational future customers.

Or consider the "Kiss & Tell" program from Gillette, intended to reduce men's tendency to shave less often and thus achieve that trendy "stubble" look. Documented by a survey showing that many women do not like stubble, the campaign included a YouTube documentary (with a variety of tips on kissing), a microsite (where couples provided kissing feedback at kissandtellus.com) and live events (like a most-kisses-in-a-minute challenge). The campaign undoubtedly reminded many women about a memorable moment when stubble got in the way—and the story that surrounded it.

A Signature Story Can Be Borrowed

Sometimes the best, most relevant signature story is not now available in your organization. Perhaps you need an inspirational story built around a set of values or a program that is not yet in place. The solution is to look to role models and their signature stories. Borrow them or even adapt them for your own.

An executive, for example, can advocate for a customer-centered service program as consistent and liberating as that shown in Nordstrom's signature story about the salesperson who took back the worn tires. Or, as illustrated by the L.L. Bean story, a firm can find the discipline to repair defective products and the innovative drive to fix problems in general. Or an organization can find inspiration to create programs that touch and improve others' lives, as seen in the story of charity: water. Even though these stories are not from your organization, they can still guide and inspire.

Consider the case of Marc Benioff, the founder and CEO of Salesforce.com, who introduced a social-good philosophy into the business model of the firm.[5] Over 100 other firms have adapted his core higher-purpose ideas and signature stories.

Benioff was in his mid-30s and one of the top executives at fast-growing Oracle when he wanted time to reassess, and to find meaning in his life beyond superficial success measures. He decided to take a sabbatical that involved a move to Hawaii and ultimately a decision to spend two months in India. Inspired by the Indian spiritual leader Mata Amritanandamayi (called the "hugging saint" because she warmly embraces all she meets), he became convinced that doing business and doing good need not be a choice—that it was possible to do both, to have a public-service mission built into a firm's purpose and strategy.

When he returned home, he helped start Oracle's Promise, designed to provide networked computers to disadvantaged schools. (It was modeled after General Colin Powell's America's Promise, aimed at fostering a greater commitment among the nation's youth to doing good.) In one project, when few employees showed up as planned to help wire a school, Benioff realized the need for a real commitment from businesses and their employees.

Thus, in 1999, when he started Salesforce.com to introduce cloud computing to b-to-b service software, he ensured that organizational commitment to social programs was built into the for-profit business model. To find role models, he looked at firms that had effective social/environmental programs. Taking the best of what he learned, he developed his 1-1-1 system: The organization annually gives 1 percent of employees' time (during the first 18 years, over two million hours have been donated), 1 percent of its product (31,000 nonprofits have benefited from software) and 1 percent of its equity (resulting in over $160 million in grants). Each of these components, especially the time commitment, provides content for powerful, higher-purpose signature stories involving individual employees.

Salesforce.com has aggressively invited other firms to join in the "pledge" to give back by using the 1-1-1 formula. The 100-plus firms that have accepted the challenge did not have to reinvent the core higher-purpose system. For many of these firms, Benioff's signature story of his journey has been a continuing part of their motivation.

A borrowed signature story can also come from news accounts, historical events, biographies, novels, fables, TV shows or movies. Whatever the source, the stories must communicate the strategic message in an intriguing, involving and authentic way. Recall the "Lawrence of Arabia" story and how it refocused and re-energized Columbia Pictures Entertainment. Finding a story unrelated to your industry or even to your customers can provide a new and persuasive perspective. And if the story is already well known, it may not need a ponderous retelling or expensive presentation.

Peter Guber also tells a story about Bill Clinton, a master storyteller in his own right.[6] Clinton was at a low point in his 1992 campaign for president, having lost the New Hampshire primary. He needed $90,000 in 24 hours to keep going to the next state. His staff asked for Guber's help. Given the laws, that meant getting 90 people to donate $1,000 each. To gain reassurance that Clinton had a chance, Guber asked to speak with him. Clinton got on the phone and asked, "Have you seen the picture 'High Noon'?"

That was it. Clinton didn't have to repeat the well-known story of that 1952 movie. In the film, Will Kane (Gary Cooper) retires as marshal of Hadleyville, New Mexico, and plans to leave town with his new bride, Amy (Grace Kelly). But he puts his plans on hold after learning that Frank Miller, a criminal he had sent to prison, has been set free and is arriving on the noon train to exact his revenge. Kane feels a morale duty to face him and tries to recruit help among the townspeople who had previously exhibited respect and support for him. But they turn cowardly, and he must face the Miller gang alone. He wins the day, but his resentment of his former supporters remains.

The message, of course, is that loyalty is needed not only in good times but also when the going gets tough. The same could be said of

Clinton's campaign and its need to survive in the short run if it was to succeed over time. His supporters could not be fair-weather friends. The "High Noon" story makes this point in a dramatic story of courage and high ideals. Guber was sold on the spot, and he used the story to get his friends on board.

Challenge: Preparing Organizations to Use Signature Stories

There is little doubt that facts without a story do not work. They do not gain attention, stimulate social activity, persuade or inspire. Stories work even though they are indirect and inefficient—or maybe because of those traits. So why don't organizations buy into signature stories and commit to them? How to get them on board? Two initial steps are to understand the power of stories and to find organizational support for developing and leveraging them.

Making them believe. There is a huge bias toward a presentation of facts, as noted at the outset. Most communication objectives involve lists of facts. Further, there is an implicit assumption, particularly prevalent in b-to-b and high-tech firms, that customers have the motivation and ability to process facts because customers are rational and interested in making the right decisions. This assumption is almost always wrong. Too often, people don't care about your offering, brand or organization. They may have little interest or motivation or even the ability to process factual information and cannot be bothered to make "optimal" decisions. Yet the assumptions linger.

The task is to demonstrate vividly the power of stories in the context of your brand and offerings. One way is to look at role models—other organizations that have used stories effectively. Another is to get some existing stories on the table, where their power to make a point becomes obvious. Still another is to perform an experiment in which a signature story communicated either to employees or to customers is compared to the presentation of facts. The measures of interest—like attention to the message or changes in perceptions and behavior—will yield eye-opening results.

Finding and leveraging stories. Even when an organization tries the signature-story route, it sometimes can't find or create the right stories. When great stories appear, they slip through their fingers or are not leveraged internally or externally. There is no mechanism for grabbing them, tailoring them for a communication role, creating a professional-quality depiction of them and then using them effectively inside the organization or in the marketplace.

Creating a context in which signature stories thrive can mean fundamental transitional changes. Such changes, of course, are never easy. Organizations that have made signature stories an important part of their communication effort provide some possible guidelines:

- Develop a set of strategic messages based on a well-defined brand vision, customer value proposition, your organizational values and your business strategy.
- Have a key executive, perhaps the chief marketing officer, commit to strategic stories and resource them.
- Listen obsessively to your customers—and to their stories of how they use your products or services.
- Offer incentives to employees to identify potential signature stories.
- Know your organization's heritage and adapt it to the issues of the day.
- Identify some signature-story role models who work in your organization and in others.
- Have organizational structures and processes supported by a staff that can find and curate appropriate stories and design profession presentations.

Create a storytelling culture. Have you ever attended a four-hour meeting with plenty of dense PowerPoint slides but not one story? No presentation that has a story to illustrate. This experience suggests a culture issue. One firm devotes ten minutes of each meeting for people to share stories. Another asks each presenter to start with a story. The result is not only a more interesting and memorable session, but employees that learn to become storytellers, a skill that a makes them more effective communicators and leaders.

There is not always a single signature story. The next chapter introduces sets of signature stories and discusses the enhanced power and challenges that they create. The succeeding three chapters cover how signature stories create impact with their strategic message: Chapter 3 shows how signature stories enhance brand visibility and energy—and why that is so important. Chapters 4 and 5 consider how signature stories persuade and inspire employees and customers.

Chapter 6 describes the prime audience groups—customers, employees and executives—and the role that signature stories play in reaching them. Chapter 7, on sources of stories, and Chapter 8, on making stories strong, address practical implementation issues. Chapter 9, on personal signature stories, changes the context from an organization to your own career and life.

2

SETS OF SIGNATURE STORIES

"The strength of the team is each individual member. The strength of each member is the team."
—Phil Jackson, winner of 11 N.B.A. titles as a coach

Skype Connects

The strategic message of Microsoft's Skype is that its power to connect users visually and verbally lets them do things together that would not otherwise be possible—*if* they think outside the box. The communication goal is to demonstrate how Skype enables creative approaches to seemingly impossible situations.

- A music conductor in New York was attracted by the talent among subway musicians there. How to harness and expose that talent? Create a symphony played by 11 subway musicians, each in his or her usual location but heard and visible to the conductor via Skype on 11 laptop computers, each resting on a folding chair. The story was told in a video and an advertisement.

- After 12 years teaching Pilates in Georgia, Denise Posnak moved to New York, but she wanted to keep training her Georgia clients. What to do? Skype was the answer. Using it, she could teach those clients from her New York base or wherever she was traveling. In fact, the clients' experience improved. They no longer needed to drive to the sessions or wear fancy workout attire, and their comfortable home environment engendered a more efficient workout. Clients who traveled could tap in from wherever they happened to be. (One was in a different place each week.) With this new operating method, Posnak is now teaching people around the world.

- Sarah from Indiana and Paige from New Zealand were each born without half of a left arm. Their mothers wanted them to get to know each other, but how to have a relationship when so far apart? The solution? By using Skype to connect daily, the girls were able to share their experiences and create a deep friendship. Skype later brought the two girls to New York, where they had an emotional meeting. The Skype story of Sarah and Paige received over 42 million views and over 3,000 press mentions, plus exposure on television, including Katie Couric's talk show.

Together, these stories tell the basic story that Skype enables creative people to do amazing things, some life-enhancing and others life-changing. They provide a message that a single story cannot.

Signature-Story Sets, Telling the Same Strategic Message

Signature stories rarely stand alone. They usually come in sets. As we shall see, there are two advantages to having sets of stories. First, companion stories add interest, energy and visibility. Second, a story set can express the depth and breadth of the strategic message, which may be too much for one story to convey.

Here, we will consider sets of signature stories with the same strategic message. Later in this chapter, we will discuss story sets that contain different strategic messages because of differences in the product, application, culture or customer type.

Sets of signature stories with the same strategic message come in many forms, and with varied rationales. Some elaborate the master signature story. Others accommodate different applications, spokespersons, perspectives or plots. The challenge is to manage the sets so that they collectively provide additive power synergistically. Toward that end, each needs a role, and the stories should be held together by some commonality beyond the strategic message.

Elaboration stories. A master story can be elaborated with other stories that add depth and interest. A certain aspect of the story—a character or a location, for example—can be the hero of a supporting story.

The Tesla growth story was elaborated by a host of stories. Those included the construction of an enormous assembly plant in Fremont, California; a distribution channel in which customers could pick up their cars in Fremont and take a factory tour; the build-out of charging stations; the creation of a battery plant in Reno, Nevada; and the features in the Model S that enhanced the driving experience.

The Molson mountain hockey rink story was elaborated with stories about each winning participant. These added texture and emotion to the master story. There was Vitaly, whose father, Andrei, was a hockey-loving Estonian who moved his family to Canada 17 years earlier and dreamed that his son, then 12, would play hockey there. Vitaly had success as a player, becoming a member of the Quebec Major Junior League with his father by his side, watching every goal. Molson set out to help Vitaly thank his father in the most Canadian way possible, by playing a one-on-one game on the "top of the world" rink. The video describing that event got 1.3 million views. Another signature story told of the actual building of the rink, fascinating for anyone intrigued by "big" construction.

For L.L. Bean, a stream of stories about Leon Bean supported and expanded customers' understanding of his persona, lifestyle and passion for innovation and the outdoors. Stories about his fishing adventures and expertise, for example, often appeared in the L.L. Bean catalog. In 1936, in telling a story about making fishing flies, he explained that eight flies in two sizes were all that you needed—and that you might as well call it a day if salmon didn't take to one of them. These stories added to his persona of being knowledgeable and authentic, which in turn rubbed off on the L.L. Bean brand.

Varied applications. Whether featuring a product offering or a customer, a signature story can involve an application. The story can gain depth and freshness when repeated with different applications. In the Skype stories, for example, the message about Skype's power to affect interactions and relationships was shown in different settings with different heroes.

The power of applications is also seen in the "Will It Blend?" challenge from Blendtec. Starting in 2006, videos posted on YouTube and hosted by founder Tom Dickson have shown a Blendtec blender chewing into a host of items, including Silly Putty, golf balls, marbles, cellphones, credit cards, BIC lighters and imitation diamonds. In each "don't try this at home" story, Dickson discusses the challenge by describing the object and posing the "Will it blend?" question. The blender seems to always perform and earns a response of "Yes, it blends!" The set of ads vividly demonstrates the blender's power and versatility as well as the personality of the brand: confident, fun-loving and humorous. The videos create a "Can you believe it?" reaction and have very likely achieved the most viral response of any series of ads.[1] A video featuring the blending of an iPod received over 17 million views alone. Total views during the first seven years of the program were over 300 million, all with a zero-media budget.

Different plots. A signature story can appear in different ways over time, but always with a similar message and impact. The Clydesdale stories for Budweiser are an example. Nearly every year since 1996, a new Clydesdale story has appeared in a Super Bowl ad with a different plot and characters. The ad is always among the top Super Bowl commercials. When USA Today picked the top 50 Super Bowl ads of all time, Budweiser Clydesdale commercials took five of the places.[2]

The ads are about the charm of animals—from horses to puppies—as well as about loyalty and relationships. All the commercials generate a similar emotional message. In one ad, a golden Labrador puppy from an adoption farm keeps escaping to visit his pal, a Clydesdale. Finally, the puppy is taken away in a car, but five Clydesdales stop the car and escort their friend back to their stable, where he then becomes a part of their lives. Another ad shows a Clydesdale foal and his trainer with a connection so strong that when the colt grows up to join one of the hitch teams, he remembers his trainer. For Budweiser, the Clydesdales provide a symbol that is likable, masculine, loyal and a link to the brand's heritage. The ads also provide a strong and predictable surge of visibility.

Different spokespersons. A story with the same theme can be told by different story spokespersons or heroes. The Charles Schwab financial firm used that approach when it developed jointly with CNN the stories of 12 CNN anchors, each recalling a person who had changed his or her life. The idea was based on Schwab's top customer targets being "owners" of their financial future, and on research showing that "owners" are almost always influenced by a mentor.

Michaela Pereira, for example, went back to her roots and reacquainted with a woman who, over lunch after Pereira's college graduation, looked her in the eye and told her that she should be on TV.

Without that moment, she would not have moved in that direction or found the opportunities she had. Ashleigh Banfield told of her mother who lifted the family from tough times and became a highly successful real estate professional in Canada. The rock of Ashleigh's life, she offered support but also some tough love. She taught Ashleigh to never complain about the rough spots but to take the initiative and move on. All the videos tell stories of mentorship and accountability in a deeply emotional way.

The stories were shown during the anchors' programs, in a two-hour CNN special and on an assortment of digital outlets. Schwab, as the exclusive sponsor, scheduled branded content vignettes as commercials adjacent to the CNN story content. The vignettes linked the mentorship message to Schwab and its own message of being an "owner" investor. Schwab also created its own "Who influenced me?" videos; one featured a girl who was mentored from high school by a man who taught her about investing, including the importance of setting and pursuing goals. She credits her M.B.A. and her successful start-up company to him.

The effort, initiated in January 2016, broke through the "all brokerages are the same" barrier. The brand opinion of Schwab rose 26 percent, and the branded vignettes outperformed the control ads (ads with a traditional message), getting 29 percent more on the "shares my values" scale. And analysis of the data showed that the firm doubled the number of digital accounts that would ordinarily be opened.[3]

Different perspectives. A story can be made more interesting by telling it from different perspectives. Recall the charity: water example from Chapter 1, and the signature story involving Natalia, the 15-year-old president of a Mozambique village's water committee. There are 25 additional charity: water signature stories that introduce different perspectives. One was about Paul Botoman, a vigorous 55-year-old in Malawi who is passionate about keeping wells going. The story starts in his childhood, showing the impact of a well in his village when he was

6; it moves on to describe his well-servicing training and his day-to-day life as a "borehole doctor." Another is about a young boy, Devison, in Malawi who walked to get water because he did not believe that it should be a "women's" job. Devison wasn't trying to be a hero or to take a stand; he just wanted to do the right thing. He wanted to give more time to his mother and to enable his sister to go to school.

Another charity: water signature story is about its founder, Scott Harrison. It provides a perspective that more naturally contains many of the organization's values and strategies. Harrison was a successful nightclub and party promoter when, at age 28, he observed that he was "for the most part living selfishly and arrogantly" and further that he was "desperately unhappy and needed to change."[4] Catching on as a photographer with a charity that operates hospital ships in West Africa, he realized that many diseases it treated were caused by unsafe water. He would start charity: water in 2006 on the night of his 31st birthday party, at which he raised $15,000 for the venture. (Today, thousands donate birthday proceeds to his cause.) The goal of his organization is to provide *everyone* with clean water. Among his tenets are these: All money goes to wells (overhead is covered by a separate fund-raising effort), the wells are locally run, and donors get to find "their" well on a map and see a picture and text description of it. A bold target is to bring clean water to 100 million people by 2020.

Why Multiple Signature Stories?

Multiple signature stories with the same strategic message have two main motivations. The first is to create interest, energy and visibility. The second is to provide breadth and depth to both the core story and the message.

Creating interest, energy and visibility. Having only one signature story can present a huge problem: It can fade from memory. If you have heard a story once, you don't need to hear it again. How to keep it visible?

A flow of signature stories with the same strategic message but unique variations can create or maintain interest. Blendtec, for example, would not have the ad impact it did if it had not found ways to provide fresh stories periodically. The same was true for the Molson core story around a passion for hockey. The elaborations were interesting in themselves and provided additional visibility and energy. More important, they reminded the audience about the core story.

The next chapter will detail the power of sheer brand visibility. Multiple stories provide the opportunity to enhance or even grow the visibility of the core story and the brand. The Skype stories keep the basic strategic message alive; it doesn't recede into the background or become forgotten. They also remind people of the general content of prior ads and perhaps even specific ads. The series of charity: water stories adds interest, energy and visibility in part by introducing new characters and perspectives.

When stories work, the early ones provide motivation to attend to later ones. They pre-sell the next story, thus reducing the challenge of attracting attention. Each Blendtec ad, with its humor and outrageous, tongue-in-cheek experiment, makes people look forward to the next one. Similarly, each Clydesdale ad from Budweiser adds to the expectation of the next.

The challenge with multiple variations, of course, is to avoid having the stories become repetitive, tiresome or even irritating. If the Blendtec ads were portrayed as serious experiments, the challenge would be greater. Instead, the humorous overlay and the obvious overacting vastly reduce the risk. In effect, the audience is in on the joke.

One other observation: There is much to be said for compact stories—those that can be communicated in a single page or a short video and are not overwhelming in scope. People are more likely to spend time on a one-page or even a one-paragraph story, or on a three-minute (or even shorter) story video. In this digital age, attention spans are short. A few compact stories are easier to process and more likely to attract attention than a larger, more complex one.

Providing depth and breadth to the message. This is a second motivation for a story set. The Molson core story gains depth and texture from the supporting stories around the mountain ice rink and the people who used it. The resulting aggregate story is thus more memorable and has more impact. In the charity: water stories, the new characters and perspectives provide a deeper understanding of a water problem and how to make progress toward a goal.

Multiple executions also allow the breadth of the strategic message to emerge. In the Skype example, it would be challenging for a single story to achieve the overall message that Skype provides ways for creative people or organizations to link with others. But with three or six or a dozen such stories, the basic point becomes more credible. The Blendtec strategic message becomes more persuasive, too, as it is replicated with different challenges.

Multiple Strategic Messaging

Some sets of signature stories involve multiple strategic messages. An organization might have many business units defined by products, applications, customer segments or countries. Some firms might have well over 100. For them, a single global strategic message would not be optimal or even feasible. Instead, they need a strategic message and accompanying signature stories tailored to each business unit. This need is particularly prevalent in b-to-b contexts, where the same brand is often the driver of diverse business units.

IBM Watson Health, introduced in Chapter 1, is in this category. It serves care managers, physicians and hospital administrators and is involved in numerous categories such as genomics, oncology, care management and personalized health management. Each area might need its own strategic message and its own signature story or stories.

Prophet, the brand and business strategy consulting firm with which I am associated, has developed dozens of signature stories to communicate the power of its offerings to prospective clients, and it adds to the list regularly.[5] Over 200 more stories are available for employees to use for their articles, talks and client pitches. Many of these stories have both one-page and multipage versions, and some have videos as well. The stories reflect different strategic messaging because the scope of Prophet's offerings is broad. It encompasses the dimensions of the practice, which is organized into three platforms: Brand and Customer Experience, Digital Transformation and Growth Acceleration. The stories represent a variety of disciplines and methods such as segmentation, brand strategy, analytics, design, culture and innovation across industries like retailing, financial services, health care and b-to-b products and services.

Each Prophet case study has a description of the challenge facing the client, the process of finding a solution, the solution itself, and a result assessment. Among the case studies were these:

- Crate and Barrel. After several years of disappointing performance, it wanted to clarify its brand and energize store traffic and sales. Segmentation research led to a focus on an underpenetrated, high-value segment—and the firm repositioned the brand, offered new products, optimized its product mix, developed new marketing campaigns with a social media component and initiated a store redesign project. After 12 months, the changes resulted in significant improvement in traffic and sales.
- The Cosmopolitan of Las Vegas. A new entrant in an overcrowded market, this casino-resort needed to carve out a niche with only 15 months to go before its December 2010 opening. The solution was to transform the casino-resort experience by redefining luxury for the Las Vegas market—to resonate with

"people who feel at home all over the world." The experience that emerged was contemporary, authentic, energizing and welcoming. The results? Among the highest average occupancy rates on the Strip and several "hot list" hotel awards.

- T-Mobile. In 2011, it was losing the fight against AT&T, Verizon and Sprint, and employees were uninspired. Research showed that people were angry and frustrated with wireless carriers in general, with their two-year contract commitments, usage restrictions, what was regarded as confusing pricing and failure to reward customer loyalty. That became an opportunity for an aggressive underdog like T-Mobile. The idea was to reinvent the category by offering its "Un-carrier" program, whose simplicity, fairness and value created a marketplace buzz and energized its employee base. The program showed that T-Mobile was willing to change radically its relationship with customers—and that it had their interests at heart. It attracted over four million net customer additions during 2013, and Fast Company named it one of the Most Innovative Companies of 2014.

- Marriott. Chinese tourists in the United States (nearly two million in 2014) were becoming an important and fast-growing market segment for this hotel company.[6] So Marriott wanted to differentiate its Chinese guest program, called Li Yu (meaning "service with courtesy"), by moving beyond common services like offering tea and slippers in the room. Research on guest experiences and expectations led to new services. One, introduced in 2016, was a WeChat program enabling Chinese visitors to speak in their own language with a local concierge. Another was a re-do of the brand graphics and visuals that communicated the various Li Yu services.

Challenge: Signature Story Overload

Organizations that believe in signature stories and find successful ways to leverage them face another risk: story overload.

Having multiple signature stories is a good thing. They can provide freshness, energy, visibility, depth, breadth and texture. In fact, most organizations need several stand-alone signature stories as well as multiple signature-story sets. But there is a tipping point after which there are too many signature stories for employees to manage or for customers to grasp.

In an organization, executives and managers use stories best when those stories are at their fingertips. When there are one or two great signature stories, they are highly visible. Sometimes, one or two is not enough—but 15 or 30 can be too many. The good ones will be ignored or hidden, and even the great ones will be under-resourced and under-leveraged because they can become buried, too. As a result, few if any are ever used or gain impact, and managers feel overwhelmed as they search for the needle in the haystack. That is story overload.

Exposing too many signature stories to a target audience—whether employees or customers—also risks saturation. The stories, compelling though they may be in limited doses, fail to gain attention or are turned off. Audiences tire of the message or the story plot and can even become annoyed. The stories stop delivering rewards in the form of entertainment, information or reinforcement of a self-image. That is also story overload.

What can be done about overload? Multiple strategies can be helpful. They are designed to ensure that all stories have a role to play and are qualified, prioritized and accessible.

Screening. Signature-story overload is often accompanied by poor screening. Put simply, some stories don't qualify as great or have a useful role going forward, so they should never make the list. If they do, the danger of overload rises.

Chapter 8 discusses screening criteria in more detail. But, in general, it all goes back to the definition of a signature story. Are the available stories intriguing, authentic and involving narratives (versus sets of facts) that communicate a strategic message? The stories shouldn't just barely qualify on each count; they should spike in all criteria.

The power and value of a signature story may change over time. Technological change may make it feel dated, or other stories may emerge that make it less needed. Some signature stories have a limited life because they are topical. The power and message impact of a signature story should be evaluated continuously—and when a decline is seen, the story's priority level and resource support should be adjusted.

Keeping it fresh. A signature-story set with a single strategic message must be timed carefully, so that each story says "welcome back"—and doesn't make the viewer sigh "not another!" That means the new story must be truly fresh and compelling.

Blendtec and Budweiser regularly offer new stories that can keep viewers involved and provide material worth passing along. Blendtec was successful in developing new stories for its "Will It Blend?" challenge, all with tension and "surprise." Budweiser, with its annual Super Bowl rhythm, reminds and rewards its loyal followers with an expected warm and touching tale.

It's important to have a cadre of story "fans" who are motivated by outstanding, arresting content. If the fresh content is up to their expectations, they will stay on board, and their enthusiasm will create social media energy. It always comes back to content. A signature-story series cannot just coast.

A lead or priority story. It is unrealistic for all stories to gain great traction, so one or more need to take the lead position. For Blendtec, one of the lead or priority signature stories that went viral involved the blending of the iPod. Most remember the iPod story because the product was so popular and the idea of blending it so outrageous. The Skype stories about Sarah and Paige were a lead story because they received enormous exposure. It is important to recognize lead stories as early as possible and to support them.

For Prophet, a few of the signature stories were high priority because of their power to communicate the strategic message. One was the T-Mobile story about redefining its industry with its "Un-carrier" program. The story demonstrates Prophet's capability with respect to business transformation, branding and customer experience. Another is the story of the Cosmopolitan of Las Vegas, which succeeded in a very competitive hotel environment in part because of Prophet's capability in service innovation and in creating and implementing a brand vision.

Prophet devotes resources and energy to ensuring that its priority signature stories get exposure. The story presentation involves a visible announcement (jointly with the client if possible), podcasts, articles, a campaign to create press coverage and a video (including client comments) that is available on YouTube, the Prophet website and elsewhere. Internally at Prophet, after a priority signature story is introduced with intranet promos and blog posts, it becomes a story resource and part of the culture-building effort.

A composite story. Another approach is to develop a composite story that includes much detail of the individual stories but may sacrifice some of the drama. The composite story might represent a "typical customer" and incorporate some of the experiences of several. The charity: water organization has an animated video that tells a composite story of the many people affected by the arrival of fresh, clean water. The animation illustrates the major experiences of many village families before the well's arrival: how women and girls walked for hours with pails on their heads, only to reach water that was often contaminated, and how girls' school attendance suffered. It then shows the arrival of the well, and the positive changes it brings. The story opens by saying that a billion people lack access to clean water; facts are then sprinkled throughout.

Synergy. Together, a group of overlapping stories should provide more depth and impact than any single story can do on its own. In the Molson example, the elaboration stories about passion for hockey add richness, emotion and depth. The same is true for the L.L. Bean stories about Leon Bean's passion for fishing and the outdoors. The Clydesdale stories for Budweiser also build on one another and reinforce the emotional connection. (Additional synergy comes from video-based stories about the Clydesdales themselves and the remarkable farm where they are raised and trained.) In all these cases, the stories are synergistic; the set becomes more than the sum of its parts.

A story bank. Another way to deal with overload is to create a story bank for employees who use stories. The bank must be easily accessible, and the stories should be coded so an employee can find the most appropriate. Prophet, for example, allows story-bank users to filter stories for a wide variety of dimensions, including industries (55 options), offering categories (11 options), time frame (recent or over two years), format (one-page, multipage, video) and client.

A story bank can also help website visitors find the most helpful stories. Skype, for example, has put stories into 15 compartments including acting, art/design, beauty, education and food. And Skype for Business has its own set of over 130 signature stories that can be searched by industry, product or language.

The next three chapters consider the ability of signature stories to deliver on three basic tasks of building brands and relationships: gaining visibility and energy for the brand, persuading and inspiring.

SIGNATURE STORIES CREATE BRAND VISIBILITY AND ENERGY

"Passion is energy. Feel the power that comes from
focusing on what excites you."
—Oprah Winfrey

Red Bull—the Astonishing Feats

Red Bull, the high-energy (high-caffeine) drink, has created a brand that did over $6 billion in global sales in 2015. It gets its brand visibility and energy from a host of exclusive events, often involving unusual and sometimes astonishing feats. For example, in its Flugtag competition, held annually in cities worldwide since 1992, participants with homemade, human-powered flying machines try to fly off a pier 20 to 30 feet high. The winner is judged on distance (the record is 258 feet, set in 2013 near Dallas), creativity and showmanship (the designs would do well in the Rose Bowl parade). The highlights video is a Red Bull signature story and has been seen by well over 10 million on YouTube and many more on the website and elsewhere.

The most spectacular Red Bull event story was a live presentation of Felix Baumgartner rising more than 24 miles above the New Mexico desert in a 55-story-high, ultrathin helium Red Bull Stratos balloon, jumping off and reaching a record-breaking 843 m.p.h. during a nine-minute fall before landing safely. Some eight million saw a live view of the event, and tens of millions more have seen it on YouTube. There were companion stories on elements of the project, including the preparation for the event and the aftermath.

Knorr Soup—Love at First Taste

The key value proposition of Knorr soup is flavor, and its brand team wanted millennials, especially, to get the message.[1] The brand needed a signature story that would travel—by activating millennials' social networks.

Its #LoveAtFirstTaste program was based on a 12,000-person survey. In it, 78 percent of respondents said they would be attracted to someone who shared their flavor preferences, and one-third worried that a flavor mismatch could doom a relationship. The provocative idea that flavor preference could influence love was then tested in an experiment. People were asked to have a foodie date with someone they had not previously met but who had a similar flavor personality, as measured by a digital Knorr flavor profiler. The proviso was that they had to feed their partners—no eating on their own. A video of seven participating couples offered fun, humor and many tender moments. Even a kiss. One supporting video included a behind-the-scenes look at the project; another recorded a follow-up date with one of the pairs. There were over 100 million views on all platforms, and well over a billion exposures among other media outlets that picked up the story. Purchase intent among millennials grew 14 percent in the top 11 markets in just a few months.

Always—Like a Girl

For three decades, Always, the feminine-products brand, engaged in puberty education but realized that its effort needed energy and a way to reach a new generation of women. The program's linchpin idea—to empower girls during a time in their lives when confidence and self-esteem can be low—would be shown by redefining the term "like a girl."

The effort began with a three-minute video featuring various people, including three young women, being asked to act out running like a girl. The results were a caricature of girls—running with heels up and out, worried about hair and generally being awkward and unathletic. Then participants saw a video of how three 10-year-old girls responded to a similar request—by running vigorously in a clearly confident, enthusiastic and very athletic way. Many viewers could take pride in the young girls' attitude.

As a result, the three young women changed their perspectives. One of the young women reflected that the phrase could make girls feel weak instead of strong. The second asked why "run like a girl" couldn't mean winning the race. The third wanted to redo her run—this time running like herself. The video ended with a challenge "to make #LikeAGirl mean amazing things" and to "join us to champion girls' confidence at Always.com."

The video had more than 60 million views in the United States and over 25 million elsewhere. A survey showed that before the Always campaign, just 19 percent of 16- to 24-year-old women had a positive association toward "like a girl." After seeing the video, however, 76 percent said they no longer saw the phrase negatively. Furthermore, two of every three men who watched it said they would now think twice before using the phrase as an insult.

The video, with its set of signature stories, is the cornerstone of a continuing #LikeAGirl campaign involving a social media effort. Succeeding videos included one featuring Karlie Harman, who became a quarterback for her youth football team. There was a "tweet amazing things" program and a Super Bowl ad that condensed the original video.

Why Signature Stories?

Signature stories are ideally suited to provide visibility and energy to brands because they can attract attention, draw people in and provide a reason to pass the story along. A set of facts that isn't clothed in a story rarely has that potential, even if presented in an interesting or even compelling way. And visibility and energy are powerful drivers of brand strength—more powerful than many assume.

Why Visibility?

Visibility is a potent brand asset. People like the familiar. Experiments have shown that even for a stimulus such as a Greek word, a musical segment or a photograph of unfamiliar scenes, simple exposure increases liking. The connection can even happen subconsciously.

The most important role of visibility, however, is to help make a brand relevant—to be considered—for a given application. Relevance requires brand awareness and credibility. Visibility drives both.

Brand awareness means that the brand should come to mind when considering possible ones to buy. A visible brand has a better chance of making that list. As visibility falls, the chance of being forgotten rises.

Visibility also creates or enhances credibility. People assume that if they see a brand often—or more often than competing brands—it is probably accepted by the marketplace and thus can deliver on its promise. As a result, the brand is included in the consideration set, and there is no disqualifying reason for buying it. Conversely, if a brand is unknown, doubts are raised. Visibility can also imply more than market acceptance. Research supports the conclusion that sheer visibility of a brand (whether that of a politician, movie star, product, service or organization) leads to perceptions of success and even leadership. Most people lack the motivation or ability to gather and process detailed information about what is causing high brand visibility.

Why Energy?

A brand with insufficient energy has three potential liabilities. First, because energy is a prime driver of visibility, a brand without energy may be forgotten. A boost in energy, however, will nearly always increase visibility. Second, a loss of energy can make a brand seem bland, tired and old-fashioned—and no longer a part of a customer's self-image or lifestyle. It becomes "so yesterday." Third, a loss of energy is associated with declines in key image elements like perceived quality, trust and esteem. The reality of these declines across brands worldwide is backed up by disturbing evidence.

The Y&R Brand Asset Valuator (BAV) database, which includes 40,000 brands measured on over 75 metrics in more than 40 countries since 1993, documents this decline.[2] For example, in a 10- to 12-year period starting in the mid-1990s, trustworthiness dropped nearly 50 percent, esteem fell 12 percent, brand quality perceptions fell 24 percent and, remarkably, even awareness fell 24 percent. This decline has continued since that analysis.[3] The exceptions are those brands with energy. In general, they have resisted an image decline and retained their ability to drive financial performance. An increase in brand energy has been shown to increase usage, preference and stock market return.[4]

Unless your brand is one of these exceptions, it needs energy! That energy can come from new products—provided, of course, that your business is blessed with truly original and different products that are meaningful to people's lifestyles and passions. More likely, it will come from sponsorships, events, promotions, advertising or internal or external programs. Whatever the source, the energy needs to be communicated and linked to the brand. Signature stories are well suited to help, especially intriguing ones like the Red Bull space jump or highly involving ones like the Always campaign. Each of these stories "pops."

Why are signature stories a powerful and effective way to create visibility and energy? In part because, in contrast to presenting facts about a brand or offering, these stories are good at two crucial tasks: gaining attention and stimulating "talk." After examining each task, we will address a key challenge: how to link the brand to the signature story.

Signature Stories Gain Attention

When a speaker says, "Let me start with a story," your attention focuses. But when a speaker talks in the abstract, communicating facts or programs without a story, your attention wanders. It just does. Stories fare best, however, when they are engaging from the outset and have detail that allows you to visualize and empathize.

Consider this first sentence: "It was a drab and rainy day in mid-May 1931 when 28-year-old Neil McElroy, the advertising manager for P&G's Camay soap, sat down at his Royal typewriter and wrote perhaps the most significant memo in modern marketing history." Doesn't that perk up your ears? Why the memo? Why was it important? Who is this guy? What happened to him? You notice. It grabs your attention and you want to hear more.

Stories draw people in. If you simply assert to your employees that teamwork is good for them, they will likely respond with a lack of interest and maybe even a cynical view of your leadership. They won't see your comment as relevant. Instead, consider telling them the story of one of the organization's most successful teams—how it was disintegrating until it changed its culture with team-building activities. Perhaps add a reinforcing story about a winning basketball coach who talked about the importance of a team attitude—and then built it. That will bring engagement.

In general, facts have a tough time attracting attention because customers and employees are not interested in lists of self-serving details about your offering, brand or firm. They just aren't. They are interested in a host of other topics and have a limited attention span. Thus, a set of facts is unlikely to be heard or processed.

Just to clarify, attention has two levels: One is immediate, or short-term, attention.[5] It represents the difference between ignoring and noticing ("taking a look"). How people are introduced to a story—the first sentence or the first few seconds of video—is crucial to their short-term attention. The second level could be labeled story engagement—prolonging the attention beyond the initial contact. YouTube research has found that the key to having viewers stay with a video is getting through the first 15 seconds. The two levels have distinct challenges, but they are related because a factor that can stimulate short-term attention often brings continued involvement, too.

What characteristics of signature stories increase the chances of achieving both levels of attention? There are many, but let's focus on five.

First, be fresh and different. Make sure that the first sentence of a story or the first few seconds of a video grabs the audience. Send an immediate signal that the story offers something out of the ordinary. It could portend an unusual character, plot or even presentation. In any case, it promises to be provocative—and perhaps surprising or even shocking.

Second, during the first two paragraphs or the first 15 seconds of video, create the expectation of meaningful rewards for staying with the story. Those rewards might include relevant information, worthwhile entertainment, a satisfying emotional experience or the affirmation of an opinion or a lifestyle choice. The audience needs a reason to stay.

Third, create uncertainty and suspense, as in the McElroy P&G story. What will happen next? Make people want to hear more, but ensure that there is a resolution that matters to them. Build and leverage the suspense toward that end.

Fourth, create emotional involvement with the characters as well as the plot. The audience cared about Felix Baumgartner in the Red Bull event—his backstory, the 24-mile ascent in the balloon, the decision to jump and the landing. In the Always story, people were drawn in emotionally to the video's characters about the real meaning of "like a girl." In the Knorr example, a viewer could feel the characters' initial awkwardness as they started the #LoveAtFirstTaste experiment.

Fifth, have a recognizable story type: In the Budweiser Clydesdale stories, you know you'll be seeing a warm, tender-hearted tale with those lovable horses as the heroes. In the Blendtec series, you know that a humorous moment will be delivered.

Signature Stories Spawn Social Communication

Gaining the attention of one audience also offers the possibility of reaching others—via social media. This can multiply the exposed population—and send some stories into viral territory. Passing along a signature story also enhances its ability to gain and keep attention. You are likely to spend time with a story if someone you respect and consider unbiased is delivering and/or endorsing it. That source is often putting his or her reputation on the line, so you will probably approach the story with a positive attitude.

Many research studies document the impact of word-of-mouth (WofM) communications. For example, a 2017 study of some 3,200 such communications in 17 product categories, mostly in Britain, demonstrated a significant and meaningful impact of WofM on purchase probability. It also provided insight into the importance of context.[6] One lesson: WofM affects customer retention as well as customer acquisition.

Another lesson: customers tend to be receptive to positive WofM confirming their brand judgment and resistant to negative WofM about it. For brands that compete with a customer's brand, negative WofM has more impact and positive WofM less.

Word-of-mouth communication has been recognized for its power since it was studied by the sociologists Elihu Katz and Paul F. Lazarsfeld. In a landmark 1955 book, "Personal Influence," they discussed their two-step model of influence, which summarized their research finding that interpersonal communication was an important missing link in understanding how ideas flourish.[7] In their time, of course, a person's influence potential was generally quite limited: maybe a dozen or fewer other people. But in the social media age, it can involve hundreds or thousands or even millions. Thus, the exposed base can grow exponentially. The challenge, now as then, is how to activate the network.

An activation program starts with understanding why people pass along stories. Ernest Dichter, the father of motivation research, published a classic study of word-of-mouth persuasion in the Harvard Business Review in 1966. It revealed that people had four motivations for passing along messaging that is relevant for building brands and businesses.[8] More recent research by Jonah Berger of the Wharton School confirms that these motivations are alive in the social media world of today.[9] The four motivations are these:

- **Offering involvement** (about 33 percent of the cases in Dichter's study). An offering-inspired signature story needs to be so novel and pleasurable that it must be shared. The Nordstrom story about the return of the used tires would certainly qualify.
- **Self-involvement** (about 24 percent). Sharing knowledge or opinions offers a way to gain attention, show connoisseurship, feel like a pioneer, demonstrate having inside information, seek

confirmation of one's own judgment, assert superiority or create a self-expressive moment. Retelling the Always "like a girl" story might reflect your own connection to the message and its goals.

- **Other involvement** (around 20 percent). The speaker wants to reach out and help, or to express neighborliness, caring and friendship. The Skype story might allow you to advise a friend on how to connect with faraway relatives.
- **Message involvement** (around 20 percent). The message is so humorous, disturbing, exciting, intriguing or informative that it deserves sharing. Perhaps it has a "Can you believe it?" moment, as in the Red Bull story.

When signature stories stand out as thought-provoking, novel, informative, inspiring, exceptionally relevant, humorous or awe-creating, they are likely to trigger one or more of these four motivations. As a result, they are more likely to be repeated in the social media space and elsewhere. Facts must achieve a much higher level of attention and interest to activate social activity. Would someone talk to others only about the specs of the Blendtec blender?

Effective activation of a social network involves a host of specialized tools and methods that an organization must master. Without them, even the best signature stories can fail to live up to their potential. Among these tools are creating the right headline, using key words to maximize search potential, promoting stories across various social media and motivating employees and friends to seed the social network.

Challenge: Connecting the Brand to the Signature Story

When the signature story is especially intriguing, the brand must still be linked to it. The worry is that the story will be remembered, but not the brand. How to make that link? There are various approaches:

- **The brand as the hero.** When the brand serves this role—as it did for L.L. Bean, Skype and Blendtec—the link is built-in. If you recall the story, you will also recall the brand.
- **A brand surrogate as the hero.** In some stories, the hero can be something very close to the brand. Consider the Budweiser Clydesdale stories, where the horses are such an accepted symbol of the brand.
- **A story that reflects the passion of the customer base.** Even when a story's content is far removed from the brand, a shared value with the customer base can provide an indirect link, or at least make the connection comfortable. An adult customer of Always may no longer be dealing with the identity problems of girls in puberty, but she is certainly empathetic. The Molson brand has demonstrated a passion for hockey that is shared by its customer base.
- **Supporting programs that carry the brand name.** These also create a built-in connection. Consider Avon's Walk to End Breast Cancer, in which personal stories about the event have special meaning for those who have dealt with the disease themselves or among their families and friends. Or consider the Pampers website, which for many parents is the go-to place for information and stories about baby care. In both cases, the brand is part of the program label and of the accompanying stories.
- **Prominent display of the brand as a story sponsor.** Simply and relentlessly putting the brand name on the signature story can be especially effective when the audience is truly engaged in a story's message, as in the Always example.
- **Adjacent communication.** Recall the Schwab-CNN partnership in Chapter 2, where Schwab commercials were played alongside the "Person Who Changed My Life" stories.

These provided a link to Schwab's interest in helping clients "own" the investing process.

The next two chapters will explore two additional tasks often assigned to signature stories: persuading and inspiring both employees and customers.

SIGNATURE STORIES PERSUADE

*"Truth, naked and cold, had been turned away from every
door in the village. Her nakedness frightened the people. When
Parable found her, she was huddled in a corner, shivering and
hungry. Taking pity on her, Parable gathered her up and took
her home. There, she dressed Truth in story, warmed her and
sent her out again. Clothed in story, Truth knocked again at the
doors and was readily welcomed into the people's houses. They
invited her to eat at their table and warm herself by their fire."*
—Jewish teaching story

They Laughed When I Sat Down at the Piano

I n discussions about the top print advertisements of the last century
or so, one written in 1926 by John Caples, then a young copywriter
only a year on the job, is always in the mix. The ad is known by its
headline: "They Laughed When I Sat Down at the Piano—but When I
Started to Play!"

This copywriter's assignment was to entice people to buy piano lessons by correspondence from the U.S. School of Music. Under a picture of a young man at a party, sitting down to play the piano, the headline set the stage for the story, which was recounted in detail in the body of the ad. The party guests ridiculed our hero when he sat down, but the ridicule turned to accolades and applause when he began to play, a talent enabled by taking the correspondence course.

The signature story delivers emotional, self-expressive and social benefits. There is the emotion of the piano player, who excelled in a high-pressure context, as well as the emotion of those hearing the story, who felt pride for his accomplishment. There is the self-expressive benefit—the expression of perseverance, talent and an ability to face down doubters. And there is the social benefit: The man became an accepted and even admired member of a desirable reference group.

This impact could never be delivered with a list of facts about the school. Such facts would not show the pride of the piano player or how he became socially attractive. If such claims were made, they would be disregarded, disbelieved or even ridiculed. But you don't ridicule a story; it's just a story.

The Persuasion Task

Why use signature stories when facts appear much more convenient and efficient? One answer is that stories are much better persuaders. They are better at influencing associations and beliefs, at creating liking and at influencing behavior and intentions.

Creating or enhancing associations or beliefs is usually considered the core persuasion challenge because they drive customer choice and brand relationships. Associations can involve more than the attributes and benefits of the offering; they can also include the brand personality, organizational values, the customer profile, use occasions, self-expressive or social benefits, symbols, signature stories and much more.

Associations are the foundation of a brand position. They address key strategic questions: What associations will resonate with customers, differentiate from competitors and be deliverable by the brand? What associations will drive a winning value proposition and innovation strategy? What associations should be created, changed or enhanced to support both current and future offerings?

Associations affect not only customer decisions about the brand and brand relationships, but also ways for customers to interact with brand—how they access and process brand-relevant information. A set of brand associations can cause information to be enhanced, ignored, altered or filtered. When a story creates effective associations, the way the audience processes additional information is changed. Negative information about products or the firm itself will tend to be ignored or treated with skepticism. Positive news about the brand or new offerings will be greeted with more receptivity than would be the case without the story backgrounds. Recall the word-of-mouth study in Chapter 3 in which current brand users were more resistant to negative WofM and more receptive to positive WofM than users of other brands.

Persuasion can affect the liking of a brand, or behavior toward it. Liking can be based on an emotional connection or an instinctive feeling that "this is the right brand," rather than on objective beliefs. In terms of behavior, the audience is persuaded to take action—telling others about the brand, visiting its website, actively searching for information about the brand, or buying or rebuying a product or service. It is behavior that ultimately affects the brand's prospects in the marketplace.

Stories Persuade More Than Facts

The persuasive power of stories has been known throughout time. Think of Aesop's Fables or the parables in religious writings that are used to make a point. Or think of the impact of "Uncle Tom's Cabin," the best-selling novel of the 19th century. One scholar suggested that its story affected the outcome of the Civil War by raising abolitionist sentiment in the North and discouraging Britain from fighting alongside the South.[1] A story that resonates can be powerful.

The alternative communication path is to present facts that lead to logical thinking and the active evaluation of an argument. As noted in Chapter 1, this model is attractive to marketers, especially those in the high-tech or b-to-b sectors, because it assumes audience members who are motivated to process relevant information, focus on functional benefits and make rational decisions. Why would anyone not be responsive to a clear presentation of compelling facts?

It turns out that typical audience members are not motivated to take the time and effort to process and analyze information. Even if they have that motivation, they usually lack credible information, memory capacity, computational ability and often even enough knowledge about a product area to obtain relevant information and use it to optimize their decisions.[2]

Further, many do not exhibit rational decision-making. The lack of rationality has been demonstrated by behavioral economists like Daniel Kahneman and others. For example, it has been shown that people will overweight potential losses and low-probability events in making decisions about insurance. And the percentage that will prefer the higher-priced of two options will sharply increase if a third, even more expensive option is added to the mix, even though few would prefer the third one. There is no rational reason for such judgments, or for hundreds of others that researchers have demonstrated.

Even with motivated people who are rational, facts can just look boring—and be hard to recall. Consider using facts alone to communicate the charity: water program of delivering clean water, described at the outset of Chapter 1. Would the statistics be noticed and remembered? More than 600 million people are without clean water? Over 40 billion hours are spent walking for water? More people are killed by disease-infested water than by all forms of violence? Dramatic stuff—but not likely to be remembered.

But a charity: water signature story like that about Natalia, the 15-year-old president of her village's water committee, lingers in the memory. It is told in professional print and video forms that are rich with detail, character development, suspense, surprise and emotion. It gains notice and influence. As noted in Chapter 1, signature stories can also provide motivation to process facts and can make them relevant and interesting.

Which charity: water approach would you attend to? The facts alone, or the facts motivated by the signature story? Which would persuade you to donate? To be a regular supporter and advocate?

Stories Affect Brand Associations

Consider the signature stories discussed so far, and how they helped position a brand by creating, changing or enhancing brand associations. The following figure lists these associations:

FIGURE 1

Signature Stories Affecting Brand Associations

SIGNATURE STORIES	ASSOCIATIONS CREATED OR ENHANCED
Charity: water	• The power of clean water for villages. • How clean water can change people's lives. • The Natalia story.
Molson	• A passion for hockey. • The "rink in the clouds" story.

Nordstrom	• Employee empowerment. • A money-back guarantee. • The "return the tires" story.
Tesla	• Best in class. • Sustainability mission—to make a difference.
Toyota Prius	• An economical engine—high m.p.g. • Affirmation of environmental concern.
Burberry	• Burberry style. • Art of the Trench—personal moments wearing Burberry.
IBM Watson Health	• The power and flexibility of IBM's Watson. • How IBM Watson empowers health care firms.
Columbia Pictures Entertainment	• Organizational units can work together. • An organization can do the impossible. • The Lawrence of Arabia story.
Skype	• Technology that connects people creatively. • The emotional story of Sarah and Paige.
Blendtec	• Blendtec's product power. • Tom Dickson's personality. • The iPod test.

Knorr	• Flavor compatibility in love relationships. • The whimsical, creative nature of the brand. • The #LoveAtFirstTaste experiment.
Red Bull	• Extreme activities and events. • The Felix Baumgartner balloon jump in space.
Always	• The "like a girl" image. • The right way for girls to think of themselves. • A brand that helps girls' transition into adulthood.

All these associations can position a brand to provide customer affinity, differentiation and strategic guidance to the organization. And the signature stories in most cases will communicate the positioning much more effectively than any assertion, even when backed up with facts.

A positioning signature story can highlight multiple dimensions of a brand and tie them together. Consider the L.L. Bean story about the Maine Hunting Shoe. It showcases the firm's innovation culture, its passion for the outdoors and its commitment to customers. In doing so, it offers a multidimensional way to approach the L.L. Bean brand and perhaps the whole category of outdoor clothing. Sure, you may be able list the values attached to the firm, but the story highlights those values as a group when it comes time to process information or consider a purchase.

Stories Create Liking

Signature stories—like those for Skype, Knorr or Molson—show that there can be a direct causal flow from liking a story to liking its elements, particularly the brand. Psychologists call this process affect (or liking) transfer. The liking of one object is transferred to a linked object. In some contexts, it is called the peripheral route to persuasion, because it is not based on belief-driven logic but on other aspects of the communication, such as whether it is liked or not.

A host of classic studies have shown that affect transfer occurs in advertising.[3] They demonstrate that liking an ad is transferred to liking the associated brand, a transfer that goes beyond that caused by the ad's content. This finding represents a significant component of advertising's ability to have impact. The affect transfer from signature stories to brands should be even more significant than that between an ad and a brand because signature stories, on average, will have a higher level of liking and emotional intensity.

Additional evidence of the impact of story liking comes from other research. It shows that liking of television programs gets transferred to the advertising within the programs and to the advertised brands.[4] Because television programs often represent stories, this research bolsters the hypothesis that story liking impacts brand liking.

Stories Affect Behavior

A host of studies have supported the idea that facts presented in story form lead to greater changes in behavior or intentions than facts by themselves. Virtually all the studies control for content—some, for example, by comparing the impact of a series of sentences formed into a story with those that are not.[5]

Consider the classic study of charitable giving by the Wharton marketing professor Deborah Small and two colleagues. In it, one respondent group received a set of compelling facts about the need for resources while another was given a story about a specific person in need.[6] In both groups, each member was given $5 to participate in the experiment. After reading either the facts or the story, respondents could give back part of the money to be used by a charity. Which seems more compelling to you? Which might engender more donations? Here are the two options:

Food shortages in Malawi are affecting more than three million children. In Zambia, severe rainfall deficits have resulted in a 42 percent drop in maize production from 2000. As a result, an estimated three million Zambians face hunger. Four million Angolans—one-third of the population—have been forced to flee their homes. More than 11 million people in Ethiopia need immediate food assistance.

Or:

Any money that you donate will go to Rokia, a seven-year-old girl who lives in Mali in Africa. Rokia is desperately poor and faces a threat of severe hunger, even starvation. Her life will be changed for the better as a result of your financial gift. With your support, and the support of other caring sponsors, Save the Children will work with Rokia's family and other members of the community to help feed and educate her, and provide her with basic medical care.

Logically, the facts paragraph should be perceived as more compelling. But actually, those in the facts group donated $1.14, on average, while those in the story group gave $2.38, over twice as much.

Other studies support such findings. The Significant Objects project, for example, showed the great value of "storified" products. It found that inexpensive items like snow globes, buttons and mysterious figurines collected from flea markets and thrift stores were sold on eBay auctions for 50 to 100 times their original cost when their collector, Joshua Glenn, had a short story written around each of them.[7]

One general research finding is that a story's impact is greater when the story is attention-getting, detailed, emotionally connected, full of imagery and relevant in space or time to the respondent.

How Stories Persuade

One reason that stories work is that they involve—they draw people in. Psychologists call this process narrative transportation: The audience is transported from its existing reality into the story or narrative. One driver of narrative transportation is the audience's ability to empathize with the story characters, to understand their experience. Another is visual imagery: The audience members develop a vivid image of the plot (even if it is told without pictures) so that they suspend reality and feel that they are experiencing the story themselves.

Research shows that when narrative transportation occurs, persuasion does, too. A review of some 132 studies reported in 76 articles from 2000 to 2013 shows that elevating narrative transportation results in a statistically significant and meaningful impact on story-consistent associations/beliefs, liking/attitudes and behavior/intentions, as well as a decrease in critical thoughts.[8] The more real the story appears, the greater its impact.[9]

Why do stories persuade? There are several explanations:

First, people deduce a story's logic by themselves. We know from research and common sense that self-discovery is much more powerful than having people talk at you.[10] What if Blendtec, introduced in Chapter 2, had just asserted that its blender was powerful and durable, even with believable supporting data? The results would be much less likely to persuade than having viewers digest a "Will it blend?" test that happens before their eyes. A story communicates 2 + 2, the path to 4. It doesn't just communicate 4.

Second, stories persuade by inhibiting counter-arguing. A story can distract from and break down suspicion. A wide variety of studies have confirmed that a story gets in the way of a tendency to confront and then counter facts.[11] Further, because beliefs emerging from the story are not contradicted or refuted, they carry the day. A story is particularly effective when there are strong prior beliefs and counter-arguing is likely. In the absence of stories, even the most compelling facts can be remarkably ineffective in changing strongly held beliefs.[12] Consider the classic study by Leon Festinger and colleagues of a cult that became more strongly committed to its beliefs even when the day passed without the predicted end of the world from a massive flood.[13] Facts don't get much more definitive than that.

Counter-arguing is destructive in two ways, so diverting people away from it is a double win. Not only does counter-arguing undercut the original argument, it also damages the credibility of the evidence or a spokesperson supporting the argument. In doing so, it weakens any future claim that uses the same source. If a retailer were to present facts about its in-store experience that were vulnerable to counter-arguing, any future communication about service programs could be viewed with skepticism because the counter-arguing pattern would likely be repeated.

Third, emotional response engendered by signature stories can affect the liking of a brand and behavior toward it. A host of theories and studies in advertising, consumer behavior and psychology support the premise that emotions are often more important that facts when consumers make decisions. In one research stream, neuro-imagery studies show that when evaluating brands, consumers primarily use emotions rather than information. Stories are uniquely suited to create or enhance emotions.

Fourth, a storyteller is usually more authentic, credible and liked than a person just trying to persuade with facts. Certainly, in the Blendtec example, Tom Dickson is more persuasive because he is telling a story.

Finally, stories persuade because they are remembered. The audience is more attentive and involved when it receives more than a recitation of facts. As a result, the content is more likely to stick. In addition, the arc of a story provides a way to organize information so that it is easier to recall. The story becomes one thing to remember, rather than a bunch of facts.

Many studies in psychology and elsewhere show that stories are much more likely to be remembered than facts, and that recall increases when the stories are more involving and emotional. Here are some examples:

- A Stanford professor, Chip Heath, gave students data on crime statistics in the United States. Each student was asked to give a one-minute talk to eight fellow students, either on why crime was a huge problem or why it was not. After a filler task, the students were asked to write down what other speakers had said. Although only 10 percent of the speakers formed the data into stories while the rest relied on statistics, some 63 percent of the students recalled stories and only 5 percent recalled any statistics.[14]

- The psychologist Arthur Graesser and colleagues rated short written pieces on three criteria: their familiarity, how interesting they were, and narrative strength. Those high on narrative strength were read in half the time by experimental subjects but still remembered twice as much as the others, while the other two criteria had little effect.[15]

- Researchers at the University of California at Irvine showed subjects a series of matched stories, except that one of each pair had a higher emotional arousal caused by subtle changes in narration. The elevated arousal enhanced the long-term memory of the content.[16]

- Many studies have shown that when a narrative's emotional intensity rises, so does the memory of the story, and the information within it. The emotion can be created or enhanced by story involvement and empathy with the characters.[17]

Framing a Subcategory

A more ambitious persuasion goal for signature stories is to position or frame a subcategory. A subcategory is born when one or more of a brand's associations become a "must have" to a worthwhile customer segment. The brand becomes the exemplar, the brand that represents the subcategory. The only relevant brands are those with awareness and credibility with respect to the subcategory market. Winning in the marketplace thus changes from gaining preference in a brand competition to gaining brand relevance in the subcategory competition. Growing sales almost always requires the creation of a new subcategory.

But how to elevate new or existing brand associations to "must have" status and thus change what people buy? It's a difficult task, but signature stories are well suited for it. They can address the challenge of penetrating and resonating with the subcategory message. It can be argued that many signature stories presented here created new subcategories by elevating various associations. There was the chance to connect visually (Skype), over-the-top energy (Red Bull), exceptional blending power (Blendtec), electric power as a response to climate change (Tesla) and the social benefits of completing a piano course (U.S. School of Music). In each case, a signature story or stories helped make the subcategory-defining association visible and credible.

Consider, too, the case of Kraft's DiGiorno. In 1995, the brand introduced a rising-crust pizza—having a fresh-frozen, not precooked, crust. The innovation allowed Kraft to position DiGiorno as having as good or better quality than delivered pizza while offering more convenience and, often, a 2-to-1 price advantage. In doing so, Kraft also framed a new subcategory: delivery-quality pizza with the convenience and value of frozen pizza—and made DiGiorno the exemplar.

The DiGiorno frame was developed with a series of signature stories, offered in a long-term advertising campaign around the tagline of "It's not delivery, it's DiGiorno." The rising crust was usually connected to the story. In one signature story, a person is recruited to be a DiGiorno deliveryman—a position that requires no work. In another, four people are watching a football game enjoying a DiGiorno pizza and comparing it to a delivery pizza with an unordered soggy crust. In still another, a couple enjoying a pizza observes that they don't have to tip the delivery boy. Over two decades, the stories have kept coming, all making the point that people can enjoy delivery-quality pizza without the hassle and at less cost.

Of course, winning is not worth much if it is short-lived, if competitors become relevant by matching the elevated dimensions. So the exemplar brand needs to create barriers by some means—for example, by continually innovating and thus raising the "must have" target standards (Tesla), by having a proprietary edge in delivering on the defining dimensions (Toyota Prius) or by finding ways to instill loyalty among the customer base (Skype). Continuing or new signature stories can also play a role in this challenge.

Challenge: Keeping Signature Stories Alive

Once you have heard a story, you generally have no motivation to hear it again (unless it is "stop in your tracks" funny). So many of the best signature stories are in danger of fading away. How to prevent that? One tactic is to find "triggers," other concepts or objects that are linked to the stories and the brand and thus serve as strong reminders.[18] Among effective triggers are symbols and events.

As shown in Chapter 2, the Budweiser Clydesdales are powerful symbols of the Budweiser brand and of its signature stories that have been part of Super Bowl advertising since 1996. The stories reinforce the warm relationships, loyalty and impeccable standards associated with these horses. When an audience sees the Clydesdales, it thinks immediately of the brand, even if story specifics are not recalled. The Clydesdales are Budweiser, after all. Keeping the Clydesdales visible helps the story live on. Three hitch teams of 10 horses tour the world, appearing in hundreds of events. (Clydesdales have appeared for more than a half-century in the Tournament of Roses Parade.)

Symbols can also remind an organization's employees of signature stories. There is a statue of the original L.L. Bean boot in front of the flagship store in Freeport, Maine—and vehicles with a huge likeness of the same boot travel the country. For Hewlett-Packard, the story of how Bill Hewlett and Dave Packard started a company by making products that practicing engineers needed is vividly symbolized by the still-standing H-P Garage. When you see the garage or its image, you recall the story and the customer-driven innovation it represents.

Events can also celebrate signature stories and brands while making them relevant for today's customers. In 2014, when Apple marked the 30th anniversary of the Mac, it celebrated the original Macintosh story as well as the substory of the famous 1984 ad introducing it. As part of the celebration, Apple offered a short film, shot entirely on iPhones in a single day by 15 crews worldwide. It highlighted how people use the Mac, iPhone and iPad to accomplish incredible feats in their everyday lives. The anniversary reminded people of the signature stories around the Mac's heritage but also linked it to the products and values of Apple today.

Events can also be triggers within an organization, reminding employees of a signature story. Maybe L.L. Bean could award a copy of the original boot to an employee who best exemplified Leon Bean's spirit of innovation. Or maybe a Nordstrom event could award a likeness of two worn tires to an employee who engaged in an exceptional act of customer service.

In the next chapter, we will turn to perhaps the biggest challenge and opportunity: to use signature stories to inspire both customers and employees.

5

HIGHER-PURPOSE SIGNATURE STORIES INSPIRE

*As legend has it, Sir Christopher Wren, the architect for St.
Paul's Cathedral in London, stopped one morning to ask
three different laborers at the construction site, all engaged in
the same task, what they were doing. He got three different
answers. The first said, "I am cutting this stone." The second
answered, "I am earning three shillings, six pence, a day."
The third man straightened up, squared his shoulders and,
still holding his mallet and chisel, replied, "I am helping Sir
Christopher Wren build this great cathedral."*

Lifebuoy's "Help a Child Reach 5"

Lifebuoy, a Unilever UK brand launched in 1894 as a disinfectant
soap, is now a global brand. And it now offers a lifesaving purpose
in India, Indonesia and some other nations: its "Help a Child
Reach 5" campaign, which promotes good handwashing habits. Every
year, two million children fail to reach their fifth birthdays, often because

of diseases like diarrhea and pneumonia, the incidence of which can be sharply reduced with good handwashing techniques.

The "Help a Child Reach 5" program was rolled out with creativity and flare. Schoolchildren in class received child-friendly materials including comics, songs, games and rewards, to help them sustain effective handwashing habits. The phrase "Did you wash your hands with Lifebuoy today?" was placed on over 2.5 million pieces of roti, a flatbread, during a Hindu holiday. Dozens of videos showed the related stories of children, parents, teachers, schools and events. One observer, Leon Kaye of triplepundit.com, suggested that in terms of people reached, it was the largest corporate social responsibility program worldwide.[1]

A pivotal event in Lifebuoy's effort was a decision to start a showcase program in an Indian village called Thesgora. The test, which reduced diarrhea incidence in the village to 5 percent from 36 percent, inspired a signature story in the form of a three-minute video. In it, a father walks on his hands through fields, puddles and a stairway to the nearby temple to seek God's blessing. Along the way, we see villagers following him, playing music. Why was he walking so far on his hands? We soon learn that it is local practice to express gratitude with a special effort—though never one so difficult. The father is overcome with joy that his boy has reached the age of 5.

In a second video, we are introduced to Utari, a woman who spends time near a tree. She waters it, dances next to it, shoos water buffalo away from it, places a ribbon around it and stays with it into the night when others are otherwise engaged. Why? In the middle of the video, her husband reminds her that tomorrow is a big day—her son will turn 5. Then we learn that it is a village custom to mark a tree when a child is born, and to track that marking as the child grows up. After five years, many mothers have lost their child and have only the tree left. Utari is one of the lucky ones, and her celebration of the tree is a way to reflect that gratitude.

A third video shows Chamki, a girl yet to be born, who is projected seven years into the future as a beautiful, happy child. She thanks her mother for all those little things like reading books at bedtime but also for washing hands to keep her safe. It puts a new perspective on motherhood and attachment to a child.

The three videos received over 44 million views and helped Lifebuoy toward its goal of changing the handwashing habits of a billion people by 2020, potentially preventing 600,000 child deaths a year. But the video also elevated the Lifebuoy brand by engendering respect, liking and a sense of shared values. The videos were powerful in part because they:

- had **compelling content**. The audience is initially curious about the characters' ways of expressing gratitude, but finds emotional satisfaction when the reasons become clear. The impact is enhanced by professional-level production quality.

- described **an inspirational program to tackle a global problem.** Each video ends with the news that millions of children die before their fifth birthdays, and with an overview statement about the Lifebuoy program.

- were directly **connected to Lifebuoy** and its handwashing program. Lifebuoy's endorsement appears in all aspects of "Help a Child Reach 5," including the videos and events. The message is reinforced by Lifebuoy's heritage as a maker of germ-fighting soap.

- were **supported by a known personality.** The Indian movie star Kajol did interviews and made videos supporting the program. She encouraged people to pass along the videos to others.

A Higher Purpose and Signature Stories

What is a higher purpose? It is a purpose beyond just selling products and services to increase sales and profits. It answers the "why" question for employees and customers. Lifebuoy is not just about making and distributing accessible hygiene products; it is also about promoting healthy hygiene habits. It is about getting a billion people to wash their hands effectively. It is about a mother and a father who do not have to experience the death of a child.

Many if not most firms are explicitly trying to develop or enhance a higher purpose. For some, this purpose articulates a challenging goal for an offering or application that inspires both employees and customers. Consider Apple's purpose, still in place, that is represented by Steve Jobs's famous admonition to create "insanely great" products and by the legendary stories that surrounded his passion. Or consider Schwab's purpose to enable investors to "own" their own portfolio strategy by becoming actively involved in its management.

For most firms, an inspiring higher purpose involves one or more social or environmental goals. Sometimes an offering-driven higher purpose will also be the social/environmental higher purpose. Tesla's purpose, for example, is to create electric vehicles that will conserve energy and reduce the rate of climate change. But in most cases, there is a need for one or more social/environmental purposes, side-by-side with offering-driven ones. Walmart, for example, has an offering-driven higher purpose, embodied by the phrase "save money—live better," that exists along with a set of social/environmental purposes.

Two Higher-Purpose Challenges

It's not enough to have substance behind your higher purpose. You also need to conquer two communication challenges. One is to gain credibility and clarity within the organization, because the reason behind the higher purpose may not be obvious to employees. The second challenge is to gain credit for the purpose outside the organization, because many customers and others tend to view such programs and their communication as self-serving and without substance.

Higher-purpose signature stories are well suited to address these challenges because they often inspire both employees and customers. Inspiration involves an elevated, more intense level of impact. An inspiring higher-purpose story will usually be more intriguing, more authentic and more involving than the average signature story. The setting tends to create empathy toward characters, while the story itself discusses engaging issues and leads to emotional responses. It is a signature story on steroids—it bursts out of the background flow of information.

When based on programs and goals that directly touch people's lives, a higher-purpose signature story can build stunning levels of audience involvement. The story can motivate people to volunteer their time, donate money, discuss the story with others or pass it along via social media. Or it can involve silent support, with the latent potential to become active when the moment is right. But a passive audience will rarely be the outcome.

What if an organization addresses the communication challenges with facts instead of higher-purpose signature stories? For example, what if it simply asserts that "our brand supports science education in schools and is very serious about being green," then makes an implicit plea for the audience's respect? Not only would such approaches be unlikely to gain attention, they could also come off as self-serving and lacking substance. The brand or firm might be perceived as buying love and respect, both internally and externally, and as not interested in the basic issue. Commitment and "heart" would be unclear. Not so with higher-purpose signature stories.

The Lifebuoy video stories, with their emotional intensity, score highly on the scales of "intriguing," "authentic" and "involving."

Watching the Indian mother dancing by the tree and the father walking on his hands is clearly intriguing: What are those people doing? And why? Each video is authentic because it is a real story about real people addressing real problems. It has no apparent connection to the selling of soap, and there is substance behind Lifebuoy's commitment. Finally, the characters and emotional plot make viewers care and want to support the program. Other signature stories—such as Knorr soup's #LoveAtFirstTaste experiment or Blendtec's videos about its powerful blender—are very good, but they lack the depth of impact made possible by the Lifebuoy higher-purpose theme.

At Walmart, the higher purpose of environmental concern has a signature story attached to its birth. The story begins in the early 2000s, during diving and camping trips that Rob Walton, then Walmart's chairman, took with the CEO of Conservation International. It's easy to visualize the fireside chat, and how it challenged Walmart to become a leader in environmental programs. Other executive meetings followed, and after extended study and tests, big commitments were made. Extensive programs were introduced in areas including logistics, store operations and environmentally responsive products and packaging. The results were an amazing level of energy savings with national import and two unanticipated benefits: There was a surprising impact on profitability, led by the energy cost savings and customer reaction to the new products. And employees welcomed the alternate conversation arising around Walmart, a brand that had faced controversy over issues such as employee policies, but was now to some an environmental role model. One article was entitled "It's Getting Harder to Hate Walmart."

Signature stories can inspire by engendering an emotional connection to a shared belief or value. The Always "like a girl" message hits home for most women and many men because they can relate it to people in their lives. And viewers gain a feeling of pride in a brand that can bring an idea out of the shadows.

In a service business, inspiration can be attained by reframing the discussion from service attributes to signature stories about customers' experiences. For example, Western Union had been communicating the ease of using its money transfer system. To become more relevant to those sending money to various places, five 30-second commercials contained stories about families in Africa as well as in the Philippines, India, Pakistan and China. We learned about the recipients, saw them in their own culture and found what the money could do for their lives. The ads personalized the idea of money transfer, making it something more than a transaction to be done efficiently. The stories showed Western Union employees that they were making a difference in people's lives and showed customers that the firm understood their cultures and their relationships. There was now a higher purpose. In comparison to more conventional advertising, these stories showed 5 percent higher revenue growth.

The inspiration and respect emanating from a signature story will obviously enhance an organization's higher-purpose program, but they will also rub off on the brand that is linked to the story. Because the story can offer a strong, often emotional level of involvement, even a weak link to the brand can affect associations.

Why Higher-Purpose Goals and Programs?

Many firms believe that achieving a higher social/environmental purpose is the right and moral thing to do. For example, Marc Benioff of Salesforce.com says, "All businesses can and should help make the world a better place."[2] An economic argument can also be made—that a higher purpose can generate energy cost savings and brand vitality for an organization and contribute to a healthier business climate for society as a whole. Then there is the impact of a higher purpose on employees and customers.

Employees need a higher purpose in today's world. They need a reason to come to work besides increasing sales and profits and getting a paycheck. They want to respect and admire their firm and want their jobs to have meaning in their lives. A higher purpose can address these needs—and bolster productivity—by offering an energizing common goal.

Many millennials, especially, are seeking meaning in their working world as well in as their personal lives. They want to work for an organization that makes a difference, that leaves society and the environment better off because of its policies and programs. They want to see more than the commercial side of their jobs.

Test your organization by asking employees two questions: What does your brand stand for? Do you care? If employees don't answer both questions positively, there is little chance that you can implement your business strategy successfully. Having a higher purpose around social or environmental programs can motivate employees to care. And having those programs communicated with signature stories can provide clarity and passion.

Increasing numbers of **customers**, too, want to have a relationship with brands and organizations they respect because of shared values and meaningful programs that address social or environmental challenges. This growing segment wants to encourage and support these values and programs because it believes in them and because they represent effective action. When the shared beliefs are strong, these customers impact the marketplace with their loyalty and support.

Self-expressive benefits are involved here. Sharing a higher purpose with a brand or organization can affirm a person's values and passions. (And avoiding brands or organizations seen as contrary to a person's self-image is part of the same motivation.)

Positive customer motivation is particularly important for brands that have created or participate in subcategories defined by social or environmental issues—brands like Prius, Tesla, Method, Patagonia,

Muji, Panasonic, Whole Foods and TOMS shoes. But it is relevant for any firm that has made a serious commitment to a higher purpose, supported it with programs of substance and made these programs visible to the target segment.

Even if the motivated group is relatively small, it can still mean the difference between financial struggle and success. A small but committed group can have an effect well beyond its numbers. It can reach out to others to retell the organizational story and reaffirm the value proposition. Even customers who voice support of a brand's higher purpose but don't change their short-term buying choices may still be influenced in the long run. This can happen when new products are introduced, for example, or if the brand runs into a negative public relations issue.

There is still another reason for a higher purpose: to provide a vehicle for creating signature stories.

A Higher Purpose Enables Signature Stories

Introducing a higher purpose with meaningful programs or offerings often has a hidden benefit: It will generate or liberate powerful signature stories that touch people emotionally and draw them in with vivid characters and significant challenges—stories that otherwise would never surface.

Those amazing Lifebuoy stories exist only because of the higher purpose to promote hygiene via the "Help a Child Reach 5" program. Without the higher purpose, the story of Utari minding the tree or of the father walking on his hands through town would not have happened. Even the most brilliant advertisements about soap alone would get nowhere near the traction of the "Help a Child Reach 5" videos.

Recall the Salesforce.com 1-1-1 program described in Chapter 1. The program enables employees to create or support social and environmental causes, opening the door to many signature stories. Both current and prospective employees have clearly been inspired by the stories, and over 100 other firms have adapted the 1-1-1 program and thus generated similar stories for themselves.

An offering-driven higher purpose also can unleash signature stories. WeWork, a firm that creates workspaces with office support for small and start-up businesses, could have built its purpose solely around delivering a workplace that works—with competent and personable support staff, comfortable and stylish furnishings and well-located buildings. It would be hard, though, to think of stories based on these functional benefits. But when the higher purpose—offering platforms for creative energy— is in place, signature stories abound. WeWork has a bank of dozens of such stories, showing how firms have benefited from its creativity-inspiring spaces. The stories are organized by categories like "founded by women," "young innovators" and "work-life balance."

One WeWork signature story is about Katy Osborn, who wanted to start a new firm but needed a core creative group. So she drew upon her two sisters—one a graphic designer and the other a videographer. The three women were close personally and professionally. The firm they would open, Amelia Street Studio, a marketing and branding agency in Chicago, was named for the address of their childhood home in Akron, Ohio. One client was Be Leaf, a salad restaurant, for whom Amelia Street helped design the menu, the interior space, the website and a quirky video vignette.

For many firms and brands, especially in the b-to-b sector, strategic messages around a functional purpose are not fruitful sources of intriguing, authentic and involving signature stories. Higher-purpose programs, however, can transform a brand by providing a whole new level of story power. If your brand does interesting things, it will naturally have more impactful stories to tell.

Stories Beat Stand-Alone Facts

Here and in the two preceding chapters, we have contrasted the relative power of facts and signature stories—how and whether they gain attention, pass along content, change associations, affect liking, inspire or precipitate behavior. In Figure 1, consider the contrasts of facts and stories of the Maine Hunting Shoe example from Chapter 1. Which will have the best chance of achieving the prime objective of communicating the boot's quality? What about making that communication memorable, likely to be retold and likely to inspire employees and customers? And which will move beyond functional benefits to reinforce the brand's higher purposes—passion for the outdoors and "innovativeness"? It seems clear that the list of facts is unlikely to even gain attention, while the story can become a vehicle with lasting impact.

Challenge: Creating a Higher Purpose

Creating a higher purpose is not easy. An offering-driven higher purpose may be right for some firms (Apple, for example), but it may not fit or is too much of a stretch for others. For some firms, a convincing social or environmental higher purpose may also be hard to achieve. Whatever the higher purpose, it can be difficult to create effective, visible programs that add substance and insure against a loss of credibility, both internally and externally. The challenges are made more formidable by the sometimes-intense pressure to deliver short-term sales and profit growth.

Amid such obstacles, how should an organization proceed? It starts with motivation. Senior executives must want a higher purpose for reasons that work for them. And the organization must see its ambition as something beyond higher sales and profits and lower costs. Given a motivation, there are approaches that work:

- Look at employees' interests. What programs would stimulate their involvement? Home Depot has a partnership with Habitat for Humanity in which employees regularly volunteer to help build homes, with a focus on veterans. Lifebuoy employees have many ways to become involved in the programs of "Help a Child Reach 5."

- Look at your organization's assets, skills and heritage and ask how each can generate effective programs. Clearly, Home Depot has expertise and materials that can help build or rebuild homes. Lifebuoy has a heritage of making soap that cleans while attacking germs.

- Look beyond the functional benefits of your products and services. What self-expressive or social benefits do they provide? Why do people really buy them?

- Look to your customers. What activities would they appreciate and value? Home Depot customers are do-it-yourselfers, so they can relate to active support of Habitat for Humanity. The problem of infant deaths in developing countries is very visible to Lifebuoy customers seeing its videos.

- Look to a long-term program as opposed to a seasonal promotion. Home Depot's partnership with Habitat for Humanity started in 2011 and is ongoing. Lifebuoy is committed to a long-term mission, with a goal of having a billion people change their handwashing habits.

The next chapter will discuss the major target audiences for signature stories: customers, employees and executives.

FIGURE 1
Facts vs. Stories

FACTS—THE MAINE HUNTING SHOE	THE L.L. BEAN FOUNDER STORY
• Money-back guarantee. • Waterproof rubber-bottom boots. • Comfort of full-grain leather. • Steel shank for added support. • Rubber chain-tread bottom for traction. • Shaped foot form for comfort and stability. • Expert craftspeople.	L.L. Bean developed boots to keep his feet dry when hunting. When most of the first batch of boots leaked, he refunded customers' money. Future boots no longer leaked.

Which is more likely to

- Gain attention and be retold?
- Communicate the quality of the boot?
- Reinforce the higher purposes of a passion for the outdoors and "innovativeness"?
- Inspire employees?

6

SIGNATURE-STORY AUDIENCES

"We learn best—and change—from hearing stories that strike a chord within us."

—John Kotter, author, longtime professor at Harvard Business School and an expert on leadership and change

Barclays—How a Brand Regains Trust

Barclays is a role model for how to use stories in a brand crisis to regain trust and change the conversation.[1] The Barclays brand, which had suffered from the 2008 financial meltdown, was later damaged by accusations that Barclays and other banks had manipulated key interest rates. In June 2012, Barclays agreed to pay $450 million to American and British authorities to settle the allegations, the first of several banks to reach settlements in the cases.

The trust level for Barclays in Britain plummeted during 2011 and 2012 to under 60 percent of its level in January 2011, compared with 90 percent for its competitive set. As a result Barclays trust level was well below that of its competitors.[2] In that time frame, banking was the least-trusted sector in a global survey covering 28 countries.[3] It is not a stretch to conclude that Barclays was the least trusted brand in the least trusted sector in the UK. Barclays decided to change.

A new brand purpose. In February 2013, Barclays announced a new brand purpose: "Helping people achieve their ambitions—in the right way." The purpose had five supporting brand values, which included respect for employees and stewardship (to positively impact communities and support sustainability programs). Extensive training of 140,000 employees, combined with a purpose-driven evaluation system, changed the firm's culture.

New programs. The newly empowered and inspired Barclays employees created and led dozens of higher-purpose programs on their own. One, the Digital Eagles, is an internal group that grew to over 17,000 employees. Its mission is to teach the public about surviving and even thriving in the digital world. Among its programs are informal Tea and Teach sessions about digital coping, and Digital Wings, an online series of courses that advance people from newbie to brain-box levels.

There are many more. Barclays partnered with two British nonprofits to create Banking on Change, to address the fact that 2.5 billion people worldwide lack access to formal financial services. Banking on Change helps create and implement programs to combat financial illiteracy, especially among women, youth, and the very poor in Africa. It makes financial products easier to understand and supports the creation of village groups to help the teaching effort, aggregate the funds of individuals and facilitate credit sources. Much progress was made during the first three years: 513,000 people from 25,000 savings groups saved more than $58 a year, on average, an impressive sum given the financial circumstances of many participants. The effort has also led to plenty of inspiring stories, whether of individuals or tiny business enterprises.[4]

The saga of culture change and employee-driven social programs makes a compelling signature story. But it was the stories around the programs' clients that touched people with emotion.

New communication. In June 2014, the communication strategy changed. Product-based communication was replaced with real stories of real people that would shine a light on higher-purpose initiatives at Barclays. There were 40 or more significant programs, but the focus turned to four, including Digital Eagles, that help people navigate the digital landscape. The other three are Code Playground, which teaches youngsters ages 7 to 17 about the basics of computer coding; LifeSkills, which gives young people the skills they need to get jobs in a digital workplace, using a free in-school and online learning program; and Fraud Smart, which gives free help to people trying to keep their money secure in the digital world. All four programs were communicated via stories of real people.

The stories made a difference. Steve Rich, a sports development officer, had lost his ability to play football (soccer to Americans) because of a car accident. But he could participate in "walking football"—usually played with six to a team on a small field with no running—and again experience the joy of the sport. Wanting to help others do the same, he decided to raise awareness of walking football and turn it into a nationwide game in Britain. With the help of Digital Eagles, Rich created a website that connected over 400 teams across the country—and connected individuals with teams. It also helped Rich himself get in touch with some former football mates. He is partly responsible for the growing interest the sport has generated. There is now a national tournament.

In another story, a woman named Zena tells how the LifeSkills program helped her son Paris prepare for getting a job. First was the Wheel of Strengths, which helped identify his strengths, interests and personality traits and suggested types of jobs that would suit him best.

Then came the CV Builder, with step-by-step guidance for creating a compelling and relevant curriculum vitae. Finally, a mock interview offered valuable practice and confidence-building. The result was an interview with one of his top target firms.

Employees were inspired and energized. And customers and prospective customers changed their perceptions of Barclays.[5] From the start of the campaign in summer 2014 until early 2016, trust was up 33 percent, consideration was up 130 percent, emotional connection was up 35 percent (versus 5 percent for the category average) and "reassurance that your finances are secure" was up 46 percent. The new campaign drove six times as much change in trust and five times as much change in consideration as the product-focused campaign that preceded it. By 2015, Barclays received 5,000 positive mentions in the press, including 600 about LifeSkills.

Reaching Your Audiences

When an organization seeks buy-in for its strategic message, values and brand vision, where should it focus? On what audiences? And what is the signature story's role and value in reaching them?

Signature stories have three primary audiences. The first is the external audience, of which customers and potential customers are most important. But this first group also includes groups like community leaders, suppliers, dealers and investors. The second audience is the organization's employees, who implement the business strategy. The third audience is executives who create elements of the strategic message and can use signature stories to stimulate options and provide direction along the way.

External Audiences—Customers and Potential Customers

Existing and potential customers are the most important external audiences because their relationship to the brand and organization can affect marketplace success in so many ways. What impact does the strategic message have on their relationships and loyalty? Does the message work better than listing facts and functional benefits in making customers trust, respect and like a brand? And when strategic messaging is useful, what is the role of a signature story?

The importance of strategic messaging. It is a common misconception, especially prevalent in high-tech and b-to-b contexts, that functional benefits dominate customer decision-making. It may sound logical, but as noted in Chapter 1 it simply isn't true. People rarely make decisions based on objective information, partly because they lack motivation—they don't see the effort involved in finding and processing the information as worthwhile. Or they may suspect that the information is biased and/or irrelevant to them. Instead, they look for cues like the price level, user profiles, past experience and, often, the reputation of the organization.

A organization's reputation can be important to many customers. Their relationships with a brand and firm can be affected by their perceptions of the organization's values, motives and methods. Brands and organizations that are respected or liked will have customer relationships that go beyond a product's functionality. With service and b-to-b brands, where the ultimate relationship is with an organization rather than an offering, such customer groups can be substantial.

Strategic messaging is particularly important when it involves a higher purpose. As discussed in the last chapter, a higher purpose is increasingly influential because it can provide self-expressive benefits to many customers. Even when such an involved group is small, it can affect an organization's profitability and reputation.

The role of the signature story. How does an organization gain buy-in and involvement in its strategic message when the audience exhibits disinterest and skepticism—and when the media landscape is as crowded and confusing as it is today?

The proliferation of social media outlets, cable channels and new online sources of information has created unbelievable complexity and clutter, making it beyond challenging to break through and be heard. If an organization is to clear that sky-high bar, it will almost always have to deliver far more than the hard facts of its message.

Further, customers are skeptical, even cynical, about any organizational communication around values, mission or culture. In their minds, a strategic message may sound noble and impressive. But they may see these messages as only words, not action, intended to make organizations feel better about themselves. So, a customer's coping strategy is to heavily discount a strategic message—or, more likely, ignore it altogether.

How do you break through with a strategic message that is noticed and credible? Simply stating the strategic-message facts will be faced with distortion, disbelief and counter-arguing. This is where the signature story comes in.

The right signature story will gain attention because it is intriguing and involving. It will be believed and remembered because it is about real people. It will avoid counter-arguing because it is just a story. And it will make a point through a narrative rather than simple facts. It can go beyond functional benefits, break through the clutter and overcome resistance to an assertion.

At Barclays, signature stories' power to break through and influence is well documented. We know that in contrast to prior product-oriented campaigns, the stories dramatically impacted perceptions of trust, consideration, emotional connection and "reassurance that your finances are secure." The signature stories, with their exceptional visibility, succeeded where the functional message could not.

Remember that a signature story may not always represent functional benefits—either directly or indirectly. In fact, its usual role is to expose the emotional side of a brand or organization. For Molson Brewing, the mountain hockey rink story from Chapter 1 provides depth to Molson's connection with hockey, a brand goal. While many of the brand's existing and potential customers are not interested in the details of beer production, for example, they are passionate about hockey. And when Molson shows that it shares their passion—by building a rink high in the mountains and selecting everyday hockey devotees to play on it—the brand and customer relationships are energized and elevated beyond functional benefits.

Challenge: Gaining external exposure for the signature story. Even a great signature story can struggle to gain exposure. In rare cases, a story will go viral without any push—simply because it got lucky. (Stories with amazing content, of course, tend to be the luckiest.) But in most cases, organizations need to prime the pump with a concerted plan to expose the story to a target audience. There is no magic formula, although some guidelines can help.

First, use all available vehicles, including articles and books, media appearances and interviews, public-relations contacts, paid advertising, blogs, websites and all forms of social media. The social-media strategy should build a critical mass of interest by reaching out to employees, friends of the brand and other influencers with followings; these gain exposure for the message and provide endorsements for it. But the entire plan always comes back to content: If you push a story that is weak or comes off as a selling effort, the effort will be ineffective and may even backfire.

Second, have an integrated, synergistic effort. When communication vehicles are operating in isolation, perhaps because of organizational silos, it is hard to send a consistent message and to achieve any social momentum and synergy. Research has shown that two coordinated media will often generate significantly more impact than the sum of the same two media acting alone. In other words, 2 + 2 can be more than 4.

Third, know that a story doesn't have to go viral to be effective. Success can also occur with a reach of just a few thousand, a few hundred or even a few dozen. In some cases, the quality of the audience is more important than the quantity. A car company may be most concerned with having its signature story connect with a limited number of active prospective buyers. A b-to-b firm may find success by reaching a few key CEOs. The story's impact would thus be based on the audience profile, as well as on the perceptions and behavior it precipitates.

The Internal Audience—Employees

Communicating the strategic message internally is a key to building a strong culture that can deliver on the message's goals. It is a tough job, particularly because it involves not only communication but also commitment to the ideas. The employees need to learn the strategic message, come to believe in it, and live it.

Each of these steps represents challenges.

Learning the strategy. The first step is to communicate the brand vision, bases of customer relationships, organizational values and business strategy so that employees understand and remember them. Clarity is vital, even amid dynamic and ambiguous contexts. Employees need to have clear strategic and tactical direction, to know what decisions are "on message" and what decisions do not support or can even detract from the basic strategic message. This requires sticky, understandable communication.

Simply stating the strategic message is not enough, because it is unlikely to be processed or remembered. A signature story can gain the necessary attention and cement the information in employees' minds. Consider the Maine Hunting Shoe story from Chapter 1. To L.L. Bean's employees, it shows the underpinnings for the firm's passions for innovation, the outdoors and customer service. And it does so with a single thought thread that, once heard, is easy to understand and remember. By contrast, a simple assertion of those passions would be unlikely to get through.

Humor can help executives communicate stories to their organization—and help them avoid a lecturing persona, particularly when the issues are sensitive. Budd Cheit was a gifted organizational leader who twice served as dean of the Berkeley-Haas School of Business at the University of California before he retired in 1991. I still recall his style of gently making a delicate point with humor. He once told a story about his economics professors, many of whom could have a prima donna attitude, just like some other professors in the business school. He joked that economics professors at Berkeley-Haas completely understood why, on average, they made a lot more money than English, physics and mathematics professors: It was about supply and demand for top talent. But, he continued, they could not comprehend why accounting and finance professors at Berkeley-Haas made more money than they did when those professors were not any smarter or more productive. Just didn't make sense to them. Such Cheit stories always got a laugh, even from the targets, and communicated a part of the strategic message in a gentle but memorable way.

Believing the strategy. Employees must be confident that the firm will deliver on its strategic message and that success will result. They need to believe that the firm is serious about the message—that a strategic rationale, program substance and supporting resources are behind it. There needs to be credibility, a feeling that the message is not just words and dreams.

A signature story can provide both rationale and credibility. Think of the Nordstrom story from Chapter 1, in which the empowered sales consultant took back the used tires. It provides an extreme, clear role model for employee empowerment and a customer-centric culture. Or consider the Tesla story, also from Chapter 1, which sets out a tangible growth plan. Or the Lifebuoy story, from Chapter 5, where the substance behind the higher purpose is made visible.

The core strategic message of Starbucks is to offer a third place—along with home and work—that can provide a welcome refuge. It is based on the story of Howard Schultz's visit to Italy for a housewares show in 1983, after he joined Starbucks but was not yet CEO.[6] While visiting Italian coffee houses, he observed the pride with which the baristas gracefully and carefully prepared the coffee. It was great theater. Equally notable to him was how the patrons relaxed in the shops and conversed with one another and with the barista. It was clearly a comfortable ritual, with quiet energy. Schultz saw at first hand how the social atmosphere and a passion for great coffee drove the experience—and how the employees' social skills and knowledge and love of coffee were the linchpin of the experience. The "third place" concept then emerged. One of the key values for Starbucks and its employees is "creating a culture of warmth and belonging, where everyone is welcome."[7] The story provides the basis for that value statement throughout the firm.

Living the strategy. Employees need to be inspired and empowered to deliver a product or service with excellence. But they should also go further, by finding unmet needs and creating new offerings and breakthrough brand-building programs—in other words, by stretching toward a "big" idea. Organizations tend to allow their prior offerings and programs to become their roadmaps for the future, but an inspired work force can see where new offerings and programs will make a difference.

Employees at Barclays clearly found inspiration in creating socially relevant programs, witnessing their impact and seeing the programs celebrated in the stories of real people. The process instilled new meaning in their professional lives and created buy-in for the new values and culture. It is easier to "live the strategy" when a higher purpose provides meaning and even fulfillment.

Consider the Molson story. It inspires employees to be creative, to consider over-the-top ways to demonstrate the brand's connection with Canadians who will do anything for hockey. Consider, too, the Skype stories from Chapter 2. They engender employee pride in a brand that enables people around the world to communicate creatively. Again, it is much easier to live an organization's strategy if it can make a difference in people's lives.

Challenge: Gaining story exposure internally. Within an organization, the challenge is to have signature stories gain buy-in for the strategic message among employees and partners. Executives need to identify the stories and communicate and leverage them effectively.

After employees have been exposed to a signature story, they need only to be reminded of it. The entire story does not have to be retold to play its role. At L.L. Bean, referring to the well-known Maine Hunting Shoe story will buttress innovation initiatives. As noted in Chapter 4, a story can continue to play active, productive roles through symbols, awards or events that remind employees of its meaning.

When employees have responsibility for identifying and presenting stories that reflect brand vision, customer relationships, organizational values or business strategies, the message can become more tangible and credible. The employee who can own one or more signature stories will be more committed and motivated than an employee who is just a passive audience member.

The Executive Team—Articulating a Brand Vision and Organization Values

Signature stories are usually conceived to communicate a strategic message to customers, employees and others. But the process can be reversed. The development or review of signature stories can offer a vehicle for understanding what a brand or organization should represent at its core. Signature stories can go beyond functional benefits by providing a perspective that gives richer concepts a voice. In doing so, they take on a conceptual role in creating elements of the strategic message.

Creating the vision. A key role of the executive team is to develop or refresh a brand vision or organizational values. In approaching this task, the team may first want to conduct a "warm-up" workshop, where key players come up with signature stories. The task is to recall stories that reflect "who we are"—stories that capture the organization's heritage or approach. Some of these stories may be well known in the firm, but others may be almost invisible—known by only one or two members of the executive team. But all the stories should represent the organization in some relevant and vivid way.

Putting signature stories on the table in this way can be valuable. Because they can involve a different vocabulary and context, they suggest dimensions of a brand vision or a set of organizational values that otherwise might not surface. The process can help new concepts emerge for consideration—ideas about brand personality and energy, or self-expressive and emotional benefits. Higher-purpose signature stories can suggest brand-vision elements and organizational values that are credible and reachable but previously were not emphasized.

The stories can also instill confidence in the workshop participants. A dimension of brand vision or organizational values that might once have been dismissed as out of reach may now be up for serious discussion. A story can provide a "we can do that" proof point.

Communicating the vision. A major task for executives is to communicate their vision for the organization to employees and customers. A signature story can play a key role—if it's the right story. Chapter 2 introduced strategies for coping with story overload, including the use of a story bank to ensure that the appropriate story is at hand.

In addition, a senior executive must be viewed as a credible spokesperson. Using his or her personal or professional signature stories—demonstrating stature and other qualities that people look to from leaders—can be a good way to create the right perception. Chapter 9 elaborates on this point.

Challenge: Finding and using signature stories effectively. Executives are more effective if they use stories to communicate. But their storytelling style is often not natural, so they need motivation, discipline and time to master the art. Start by observing how the most effective executive communicators make their points with stories. Then resolve to be a good storyteller, not a lecturer or an exerciser of authority. Then make it a part of your style.

Implementing a Story-Driven Program

Believing in signature stories' strategic power and value is only part of the task. The next two chapters address practical approaches to effective signature stories. Chapter 7 explores routes to finding or creating these stories. Chapter 8 discusses the dimensions of strong signature stories, and how they can help those who evaluate, refine and present the stories to an audience.

SOURCING SIGNATURE STORIES

*"The way to get good ideas is to get lots of ideas and
throw the bad ones away."*
—Linus Pauling, theoretical physical chemist
and Nobel Prize winner

Coca-Cola's Happiness Machine

In 2009, Coca-Cola needed a way to build deeper relationships with teenagers—one that would stimulate social networks.[1] The strategic message of the effort would follow Coke's central promise to "inspire moments of optimism and happiness," and bring it home to a youthful audience around the world. The result was a seven-pronged effort, including a "Spin the Coke" app that got a million iPhone downloads.

The project also included a memorable video, starring what Coke called the "Happiness Machine." At a student hangout at St. John's University in New York, an ordinary-looking Coke vending machine was installed with hidden cameras in the room. Unsuspecting students approached the machine to buy a Coke and instead got a series of surprises. First, the machine started dispensing a seemingly endless stream of Cokes—quickly gaining the students' delighted attention. Then a hand emerged from the machine, offering a bouquet of flowers. The surprises kept coming: A balloon dog, a pizza and, finally, a submarine sandwich yards long emerged from the machine. Two students were so happy that they gave the machine a hug. Like many other moments of happiness, these were prompted by unanticipated generosity, and the fact that nothing was expected in return.

A two-minute video telling the story received over eight million views. The company employed variations on the idea in other countries, including a phone booth in the United Arab Emirates and trucks in Rio de Janeiro and the Philippines. The idea also inspired a pair of "Small World" machines—one in Lahore, Pakistan, and the other in New Delhi, India. The two countries have long been at odds politically, but the machines bridged the gap in their own unique way. Touchscreen technology projected a streaming video feed onto the machine screens simultaneously, so that people in each city could complete a friendly task together—waving, dancing or drawing a peace sign—before sharing a Coca-Cola. Videos featuring tender moments, as when a young girl in New Delhi "touched" hands with an older woman on the Pakistani side, generated more than three million additional exposures.

Research showed that those who saw the Happiness Machine video were more likely to remember it and feel connected to Coke than were people who saw a Coke commercial. And teenage viewers strengthened their belief that the Coke brand creates connection between individuals and inspires happiness. Given that the video's cost was minuscule, especially when compared with a $3 billion Coke advertising budget, the impact was remarkable.

Creating or Finding Signature Stories

How do you come up with effective signature stories? How do you stimulate the right stories, filter out others, refine the most promising and ultimately decide which ones to resource and which to elevate to flagship status?

First, know your strategic message. The Happiness Machine was inspired and guided by the Coke vision of connecting happiness with a clear target market. It was not aimless.

Inside your organization, which strategic message needs clarity or an emotional boost? Is it your values, your brand vision, your customer relationships or your business strategy? What are the priorities? Which employee or executive perceptions and attitudes need to be created, reinforced or changed to allow the business strategy to succeed? Externally, what aspects of the strategic message can influence customer relationships? What are the priorities in brand enhancement or brand activation? What are the target markets, and which ones are most conducive to stimulating growth or loyalty?

Second, allow a spectrum of stories to emerge—as Coca-Cola did. Realize that the strategic message or messages can inspire the development of a wide variety of story heroes, story contexts and presentations. Getting a lot of ideas is a way to get good ideas. Ferret out the existing stories to make them visible enough for consideration. But create a flow of new stories, too.

Developing a rich story set offers several benefits. The effort harnesses creativity, increasing the likelihood that novel and intriguing stories will emerge. And when there are multiple target markets, it is unlikely that a single signature story will be effective in all of them. The Happiness Machine idea that works on an American college campus may need a different twist in the United Arab Emirates or Rio de Janeiro. Lastly, if several signature stories are aimed at the same audience, they can reinforce one another and avoid becoming stale with repetition.

The story ideas need not be geared to a broad market or require a big budget. Connecting with the right audience of modest size can be more productive than just reaching a huge one. Coca-Cola used brainstorming to create multiple executions of its program, none of which were costly. Creative and unusual ideas were all tied to target markets, and each story provided enticing content. There was no need to achieve broad audience appeal simply to spread the cost.

Third, in developing multiple signature stories, buy into a "test and learn" philosophy. Rather than waiting for the "sure thing" story, try those that are imperfect but have some chance of being effective and see what works. If some, like the Happiness Machine story, already click or are worthy of further investment and refinement, go ahead with them. If not, back off. In the digital age, speed is vital and quick testing is feasible. You can afford to introduce many signature stories or sets of stories and let the best emerge.

Owned vs. Borrowed Stories

Signature stories have two sources. They can be based on your own firm or brand (owned stories) or can be borrowed. Owned stories are emphasized in this book because have the most potential to be intriguing, authentic and involving, with an on-target strategic message. But an ownable story that "pops" may not be immediately available, especially if the strategic message is aspirational. It may be necessary to look elsewhere for a signature story that is especially powerful and relevant, and that can be borrowed and adapted.

Chapter 1 outlined two types of borrowed stories. The first seeks role models outside your firm that have already accomplished what your aspirational strategic message represents. Recall that over 100 firms have started their own versions of the 1-1-1 program originated by Salesforce. com to address social issues. Many have also adapted the Salesforce. com signature story to inspire their efforts. The second type of borrowed story draws more widely from any source, including news events, history, novels or movies. Recall the experience of Peter Guber, also recounted in Chapter 1, who used the Aqaba story from "Lawrence of Arabia" to change the culture and strategy of Columbia Pictures Entertainment. Recall, too, the Jewish teaching story at the top of Chapter 4, about a woman who was turned away from villagers until she was clothed in a story. It is a signature story for this book.

Consider a borrowed story when ownable stories are simply not powerful or relevant enough to work. When you need a borrowed story, cast a wide net—guided by your strategic message. Think of that message in as many forums and contexts as possible. Search for role models. Go through lists of top movies or books and see if they trigger workable stories. When digesting news, look for metaphors that deliver your strategic message. A well-known story with an obvious point offers an advantage. Recall from Chapter 1 how Bill Clinton needed only to mention the movie "High Noon" to activate a signature story of supporter loyalty.

Story Heroes

Ownable signature stories have a hero or a set of heroes. To find possible candidates, consider various hero types. The goal is to find ones that are intriguing, authentic and involving; will advance the message of the brand, organization or business strategy; and will inspire employees and motivate customers.

In this chapter, 10 types of heroes are described:

• Customers	• Employees
• Offerings	• Organization programs
• Brands	• Founders
• Brand endorsers	• Revitalization strategies
• Suppliers	• Growth strategies

This list could easily grow by dozens. But these 10 provide starting points in the search for powerful stories. The beginning of Chapter 1 offered case examples of five of these hero types: customers, offerings, brands, founders and growth strategies. Those five, in addition to employees, organization programs and revitalization strategies, are perhaps the most common in effective signature stories.

These story types are not distinct; they overlap. Further, most signature stories have two or more heroes embedded in them. Offerings and brands, for example, appear in many signature stories but sometimes do not claim or even share top billing. Although many signature stories are used for external and internal communication of a strategic message, the five in the left column are generally more important to the external audience and the five in the right column are most important for internal consumption.

Customers

Customer heroes can be effective because they lack a self-serving message that "my brand (or offering) is better than yours," and their stories are often closely linked to the organization's values or the brand's value proposition. Further, there is a growing consensus that customer experiences and associated stories are becoming more important in brand-building and marketing. That is because customers value information derived from other customers' experiences more highly than information from commercial sources. This logic is especially true for service and b-to-b brands. The IBM Watson Health customer story was particularly relevant to other potential health-organization customers that were dealing with similar issues.

LinkedIn, the business- and employment-oriented social network, has a series of professionally created, one-minute stories built around the idea of leveraging the power of LinkedIn to advance a career path. Jenni, for example, told of conducting intense networking that led to a marketing position and, ultimately, supported a decision to have her own firm. Angela shared her passion for her work as a freelance consultant in digital analytics and how she solves clients' business mysteries by using math. Tim told of fulfilling his dream of opening a distillery. Several of these story videos received over one million views.

Customer stories can be observed, or customers can be motivated to reveal them. LinkedIn offers members the opportunity to tell their own success stories, and the most compelling receive a professional video treatment. A Purina Cat Chow contest asked customers to tell stories about how they related to their pets, with themes like "Why I'm a Cat Person," "How We Found Each Other," "Always There for Me" and "Memories." The stories captured these emotional connections.

Another route to finding these stories, especially fruitful in b-to-b contexts, is simply to get close to customers by interacting with them, by talking and observing. Reach your customers where they live—where they buy and use your offerings. Understand their problems and the underlying issues. Stories will emerge.

Offerings

An organization's offerings—its products or services—are often the heart of the strategic message. For example, they took the lead in the charity: water story, described in Chapter 1, where the ability to create and manage a source of clean water had a dramatic effect on the lives of the story's characters. The strategic message about the offering and its impact was front and center.

An offering is often a part of a signature story, as it was in the L.L. Bean and Nordstrom stories from Chapter 1 and the Skype case from Chapter 2. But it can also be the principal hero, as it was for the signature stories of Blendtec ("Will it blend?," Chapter 2) and DiGiorno pizza ("It's not delivery, it's DiGiorno," Chapter 4).

The classic Timex ads, also in that category, placed the company's watches in a variety of at-risk contexts. A cliff diver in Mexico, for example, undertook a scary jump while wearing a Timex. An extreme challenge for the diver and the watch. Will the watch still work? After the diver struggles to reach shore, the newsman John Cameron Swayze, here the narrator, reports that the Timex has emerged unscathed—that it "takes a licking and keeps on ticking." Such offering-as-hero stories require little interpretation because the brand is an integral part of the story.

Brands

A brand can become a story hero via programs or promotional events that are unrelated or only tangentially connected to a product or service. If so, the story must communicate brand characteristics that go beyond the offering. The Molson story from Chapter 1 communicated the brand's passion for hockey. The Happiness Machine story in this chapter demonstrates a form of happiness driven by a Coca-Cola experience. MasterCard provides another example.

MasterCard has long built brand enhancement and visibility with its "priceless" concept. It shows how people can value experiences and family connections more than things. The challenge was to inject energy into this long-running campaign by creating stories that intrigue and gain involvement. How to do that?

The effort started with customer research showing that people find more happiness in rewards when they are unexpected. This led to the "Priceless Surprise" program, in which cardholders are surprised with a visit from a celebrity, or free event tickets, or both, generating a new set of "priceless" signature stories."[2] Rewards very unlike those of other loyalty programs. In one example, a father and four sons in a sports bar decline an offer of two tickets to a big hockey game because they don't want to break up their family group; a few minutes later, the hockey legend Doug Gilmour asks them all to join him in a premium box at the game. In another example, a Justin Timberlake fan is stunned when the singer knocks on her door just to chat. In still another, at a MasterCard-sponsored concert at the Moscow Tchaikovsky Conservatory, the audience is surprised when Darth Vader and his soldiers enter the hall to hear music from "Star Wars."

Delivering such big emotional moments has made for powerful stories and brand energy. Some 260 of these "Priceless Surprise" events across 34 countries have surprised 270,000 people. In Europe, MasterCard found a 47 percent lift in brand consideration associated with the stories within the prime target audience. In Latin America, it saw an 89 percent increase in the likelihood of using the card. In Canada, 31 percent of cardholders reported that they were more likely to use MasterCard due to the possibility of a surprise. In the Asia-Pacific region, the campaign got 47 million social media engagements and a click-through rate 1.5 to 3 times the industry average.

Brand Endorsers

A brand endorser provides attention-getting interest for signature stories, leveraging his or her credibility and/or prestige. Nike, Dos Equis and Uniqlo are among many companies that have used intriguing endorser stories to bring energy to their brands.

For a decade starting in 2006, Dos Equis portrayed a bearded, debonair gentleman, roughly in his 70s, as the "The Most Interesting Man in the World." He tells stories about his daring exploits when he was younger—winning an arm-wrestling match, surfing a killer wave, bench-pressing two young women in a casino—and offers opinions on subjects like bar nuts, the two-party system, self-defense, trophy wives and bromance. The voiceovers are both humorous and outrageous. At the end of the ad, the Most Interesting Man, usually shown in a nightclub or other social setting surrounded by several beautiful young women, says: "I don't always drink beer. But when I do, I prefer Dos Equis." These signature stories provide visibility and energy by creating a personality and associating the brand with discerning tastes.

Uniqlo, the clothing retailer based in Japan, has a family of branded technologies including Heattech, which creates and retains heat; AIRism, which cools the body and wicks away moisture; BlockTech, which blocks wind and water; and Dry-Ex, for athletic activities. These technologies defined Uniqlo as an innovative retailer, offering advanced products for casual and active living, and helped it become the seventh-strongest brand in Japan in 2017.[3] But how does a firm communicate such technologies and give them visibility? It calls on Marin Minamiya.

Minamiya, a youthful mountain climber, became a visible user, endorser and adviser of Uniqlo and its technologies.[4] Her stories are legendary: At 19, she became the youngest Japanese person to climb Mount Everest, and by age 20 she had conquered the Seven Summits, the highest mountains on all seven continents, often encountering high winds and shockingly low temperatures along the way. Her accounts of her adventures, including the time she fell from a cliff and spent a night in the snow, show remarkable perseverance and stamina and moments of high tension. They also show insight and emotion. Of her first efforts, she said, "I instantly fell in love with the beautiful view while trekking, and the feeling of tranquility, peace and freedom that this mountain brought me."[5] She and her stories are connected to Uniqlo, giving new visibility to its innovation in fabrics.

Suppliers

The supplier as hero can help provide credibility for a value proposition. For food companies, for example, such stories can focus on their organic and natural product offerings. Clif Bar & Company has a series called Farmers Speak, built around starting and operating organic farms where ingredients are grown. The four-minute videos describing the first two stories received over 600,000 views on YouTube.

One story features Brian Krumm, whose Saskatchewan farm was started by his grandfather and father and had long used conventional chemical methods. Krumm now farms 2,880 acres. Over time, he says in the video, he worried about possible effects of chemical methods on his family as well as the disappearing songbirds—and in 1996 decided to make the three-year transition to organic farming. Instead of chemicals, his tools became crop rotation, organic fertilizers and the timing of planting. Comparing conventional and organic farms, he notes, "they spray; we till." He says that he would never go back, and that he enjoys what he sees as a safe farm environment for his children and grandchildren—an environment where songbirds and frogs abound.

Employees

As the Nordstrom story illustrates, employees can be a source of a strong and memorable signature story because they are on the front lines. And other employees can empathize with the story and the relevant issues it raises.

Zappos.com, the online shoe store, has a set of signature stories build around its 10 core values, one of which is to deliver "wow" customer service. One story involves a Zappos call-center employee who, in the wee hours of the morning, received a call from a customer who could not find a pizza store that was still open. Instead of gently turning away the customer, the employee found a list of nearby pizza stores that were open all night.

Employee stories often need encouragement to surface. Mobil, the oil company that is now part of ExxonMobil, built a contest around its corporate brand tenets of "leadership," "partnership" and "trust." In the contest, any employee or group of employees could nominate a person, group or program that best exemplified one of the three tenets—with the winner going to the Indianapolis 500 with insider status. Mobil received over 300 entries and some incredible stories.

Organization Programs

An organization program, often not related to the marketing of a physical product, can serve as a hero by providing substance behind the organization's values or strategy—and by serving as its representative. But the program also needs to be visible. That is the role of the signature story.

Consider the Berkeley-Haas School of Business, which has several signature stories providing substance behind its commitment to four values: "confidence without attitude," "beyond yourself," "students always" and "question the status quo." These values have served to differentiate and to inspire. One signature story involved changing the admissions process to include "value compatibility." Applicants are now invited to use three required essays (on topics like "an experience that has changed how you view the world") to reflect on how they share the school's four values. As a result of this process, the M.B.A. student body became much more cohesive (more shared values and goals) and positive (less competitive and more collaborative) than prior classes and probably classes of competing schools as well.

Founders

An organization's founder can be a powerful source of signature stories because the core values and value propositions are often apparent at the firm's origins. We saw this in the L.L. Bean story from Chapter 1. Another example is seen at Clif Bar & Company, whose founder, Gary Erickson, was on a 175-mile bike ride in 1990 when he felt low on energy. As the company says on its website, he just "couldn't eat another unappetizing, sticky, hard-to-digest bar." The experience inspired him to make a better-tasting energy bar with nutritious ingredients. And he did.

A founder story is often the breakthrough for gaining external and internal credit for a higher purpose. According to the Y&R Brand Asset Valuator, the huge brand database, the leading brands in terms of socially responsible activities are TOMS shoes and Patagonia, the retailer of outdoor clothing and gear. Both have dramatic and visible founder stories, as do many of the brands with high rankings on a social/environmental dimension.[6]

While traveling in Argentina in 2006, Blake Mycoskie, the founder and Chief Shoe Giver of TOMS, witnessed the hardships faced by children growing up without shoes. His solution to the problem was simple—start a retail shoe firm that would give away a pair of shoes to those in need for every pair sold, the One for One program. By 2017 the firm had given over 60 million pairs of shoes away and had expanded the program to eyeglasses.

The Patagonia founder story goes back to around 1970, when Yvon Chouinard, an avid rock climber who ran a climbing equipment firm, had a guiding inspiration: He wanted to make rock-climbing as clean as possible—meaning that climbers should depart the rock wall without leaving behind pitons or damage from hammers. His firm would offer the design and production innovation necessary for new, environmentally friendly products. As Chouinard moved into clothing with Patagonia, his priorities stayed the same. They are reflected in the current mission statement, which says the firm will "use business to inspire and implement solutions to the environmental crisis." Rather than gaining a sale, he would prefer that people keep using old garments, repairing them when need to save the water and energy used to make them. And the story about leaving rock walls clean still clarifies and inspires the brand.

To maximize the value of a founder story, make it relevant to the current audience. Don Julio Gonzales, founder of Don Julio, a luxury tequila brand, made several bold moves reflecting his category vision and his "put passion above all" philosophy. These were described in signature stories portrayed in print, TV and billboard ads.[7] He broke with tradition by planting his agave plants further apart, to produce a richer tequila, and by designing a shorter bottle, so people could look into one another's eyes at table. His willingness to chart his own path provided inspiration for millennials, a prime target group—and the brand's "Make Your Move" tagline reinforced the message. As a result, while the tequila category grew 4 percent in sales and the luxury tequila leader was up 7 percent, Don Julio was up 30 percent.

Revitalization Strategies

A revitalization strategy points to a new culture or path for an organization that may have stagnated or declined. But this new direction needs credibility, as well as support from internal and external audiences that often don't give it easily.

A signature story can help. It can focus on the how the new approach was born: What were the trends, new customer "must haves," competitive actions, opportunities or crises that led to the strategic message? What were the alternatives? Such a story can be intriguing, involving and authentic. Or the story can focus instead on the strategy's impact on products and services, customers, employees or others who can make the new path tangible and meaningful. Or it can do both.

Prophet's T-Mobile story from Chapter 2 illustrates. From a position of market weakness as it faced three large competitors with marketing programs like its own, T-Mobile chose to reinvent the category with its "Un-carrier" concept. Its programs offered a simple alternative to a confining, complex service model that had been the industry standard. The market responded.

Lou Gerstner transformed IBM when he became chief executive in 1993. At the time, IBM was struggling, ruled by product and country fiefdoms and poised to break itself up into seven companies.[8] Should

Gerstner proceed with the breakup of the firm? To help decide, he solicited customer feedback by having the 50 top executives and their direct reports visit five customers each. He found that customers loved IBM but wanted to be able to buy integrated solutions from one firm. As a result, he put an end to the breakup proposal and worked to make product and geographic silos communicate and cooperate on systems solutions under the global IBM brand. Some rather forceful and difficult actions were required to incent the organization to buy into the new strategy, culture, organizational structure and success measures. The background story would influence the firm for decades.

A business revitalization story can have two lives. The first is when the new business strategy is in progress but the end point has not been reached. The focus is thus on the future, with a roadmap for getting there. The story can clarify and motivate the new strategy and inspire employees and customers alike. The second life begins when the new plan is in place. The story then becomes a reminder of why it was needed, making the strategy clear and vivid in people's minds. When a strategy becomes too familiar, it tends to lose influence and inspiration. The story helps keep the excitement going.

Growth Strategies

Growth is vital to an organization. For employees, it provides opportunity and the joy of winning, and it guides and inspires programs and initiatives. Among customers, it offers the key brand drivers of energy and visibility, as well as the opportunity for better products. For suppliers and retailers, it means increased demand and price stability. In short, it means running an organization with the wind at your back.

A growth story that is intriguing, involving and authentic can convince audiences that the growth will happen, that it is real. It allows the organization to focus on a long-term strategy, perhaps by investing in assets like brands that will pay off well into the future. Otherwise, short-term financial considerations can dominate a firm's decision-making. In some sectors, even investors look to growth stories rather than short-term profits. That has been true for firms like Tesla (whose growth story appeared in Chapter 1), Amazon and others that have captured huge stock market values even if profits are sacrificed in the process.

Consider the Amazon growth story.

It is 1996, two years after Jeff Bezos left a New York hedge fund to start an online bookstore, Amazon.[9] The story starts with a foundation on which to build: Amazon would be the bookstore of choice, with over a million book titles to be sold at prices well below those of brick-and-mortar book retailers. The store's website would be personalized for each customer, suggesting books based on previous purchases. To run the store, Bezos would hire only the brightest people who would be willing to work long hours, work hard and work smart.

With this foundation established, Amazon had a goal: to grow at an insane rate to capture market power and economies of scale, and in areas far beyond bookselling. Note that he did not call his firm books.com. It was named Amazon after the largest river in the world because the goal was to be the largest retailer in the world, to become the everything store. Bezos talked of selling not only kayaks, but also reservations for kayak trips.

In 1996, Amazon had annual sales of just $16 million, less than 1 percent of those of Barnes & Noble. But Bezos had more than a goal; he had a growth story—one that he would follow for the next two decades and more. It turned out to be even more successful than he imagined.

Challenge: Finding Ownable Signature Stories

Signature stories do not just appear. They are born through a process. Recall the suggestions at the outset of this chapter: Know your strategic message, put lots of story options on the table and use a "test and learn" approach to find the right ones.

Some additional thoughts:

In developing signature stories, rewards may be needed to create motivation. Sometimes that motivation can take the form of a contest, as shown by Purina (the cat relationship stories) and Mobil (stories around partnership, leadership and trust). But motivation can also be baked into a culture's expectations, with recognition programs and performance evaluations.

The nurturing of potential signature stories should have a "bottom-up" flow, in that the stories are detected by employees. Make sure that employees involved in the strategic message are sensitized to what a signature story is—and then incent them to call in a "story team" to take the stories to the next level. The team should evaluate the stories, activate the best ones and provide support in writing and video creation. That was the case with the Salesforce.com 1-1-1 stories from Chapter 1 and the Barclays stories from Chapter 6.

The process should also have a "top-down" flow in which the signature stories are identified or stimulated by the story team. Thinking and acting like journalists, the team members should know how to seek out stories and write or film compelling narratives—and then place them in the appropriate media.

The process of developing, refining and presenting signature stories needs support from frameworks in the organization. Altimeter, the digital research group at Prophet, has found that organizations with successful digital strategies manage digital content with one or more organizational framework models. Because digital content takes the form of stories or stimulates stories, these findings are relevant to signature stories' creation and management. Here are some of those models:

- A content center of excellence: a consortium of experts who provide leadership and best practices for finding and developing signature stories and other content.

- An editorial board/content council: content creators and/or marketing executives who meet to evaluate, prioritize and align content, including signature stories.
- A content lead: a person who leads content initiatives (such as a signature-story set) editorially and/or strategically, without departmental authority.
- A content department: an in-house or agency group that turns stories and other content into high-quality presentations, using formats like advertisements, speeches, videos, articles and podcasts.
- A cross-functional content chief: a senior executive with cross-department authority to align content including stories and ensure that they are leveraged across the entire organization.

An organization must also recognize the right balance between its strategic message and a story's ability to gain attention and hold interest. Your strategic message is vital, but don't let it strictly confine the story search. In storytelling, authentic content that intrigues and involves is king. If you find stories with great content, try to make them message-relevant. Conversely, if message-driven stories are available, look for ways to punch them up or replace them with other, more absorbing ones.

Not every story is worth elevating to signature status. All should be evaluated for their strength and promise. The next chapter addresses that challenge.

WHAT MAKES A SIGNATURE
STORY STRONG?

"Tell me a fact and I'll learn.
Tell me a truth and I'll believe.
But tell me a story and it will live in my heart forever."
—Native American proverb

Creating Signature Stories at General Electric

General Electric is a role model for finding stories that resonate.[1] The firm tries out ideas, usually led by stories, and runs with the best of them with a bit of refinement along the way. Although it has some ad campaigns, GE emphasizes content-driven audiences (it has over four million members over a variety of social media platforms) rather than print readers or television audiences. It prefers to own rather than rent media.

One GE strategic message is its DNA. The message is linked to company founder Thomas Edison and his passion for science and technology, to its history as a 125-year-old startup and to its reputation for imagination and creativity in motion. Another, more modern message has to do with "digital industry"—how GE helps build digital technology into machines such as locomotives and jet engines, allowing them to communicate better with one another and with people and organizations. The target audiences are prospective and current employees, buyers in customer organizations, and those who would influence these groups. The messages also aim at people who are fascinated with science and technology in general.

Observations from the GE experience suggest several, very different routes to strong signature stories:

Bring technology breakthroughs to life. Partnering with National Geographic and top Hollywood storytellers like Ron Howard, GE helped put together a six-part documentary TV series about scientific breakthrough stories from its labs. The stories show how the company faced enormous unknowns and technical challenges but emerged with innovations that have changed lives. The series, which looked at pandemics, aging, water issues, energy issues, human engineering and improving the brain, was shown on the National Geographic Channel and, streamed on GE Reports. It reached some 170 countries.

Get personal. Mark Frontera, a lab manager at GE Global Research, saw at first hand the impact of his work after his son, Adam, then 4, was diagnosed with pediatric cancer. The treatment that Adam received at the Dana Farber Cancer Institute involved advanced imaging technology developed at a GE Global Research facility, the High Energy Physics Lab. After Adam completed his treatments, his father created a video of his story and the role of the imaging technology. It was shown on GE social media sites and on YouTube.

Connect to your heritage. As a maker of advanced materials, GE had a prominent role in the 1969 moon landing. To retell that story for the 45th anniversary of the event, GE introduced on Snapchat an interpretation of the astronauts' original moon boots, employing advanced GE materials used in jet engines and wind turbines. One hundred pairs of these moon-boot sneakers, called "the Missions," went on sale on the anniversary day at a price of $196.90. Buzz Aldrin helped with the launch by posting on Snapchat a photo of himself wearing a pair. The shoes later sold on eBay for thousands of dollars.

Play to your audience. GE knew instinctively that its target audience was fascinated with big machines and how they work—and would thus love to visit its factories. So, six Instagram influencers and six GE super-fans were sent to a jet engine test site in rural Ohio and were asked to record the experience. More than a dozen other visits were also arranged—to sites ranging from Texas to Norway. The results were shown to GE's social media audience members and on other social media sites. The first #GEInstWalk video received some 200,000 views within 48 hours.

Offer user-generated content. GE partnered with "The Tonight Show Starring Jimmy Fallon" for a series of eight-minute segments, called "Fallonventions," in which young people presented their clever inventions. (One allowed people to reach Pringles chips low in the package by inserting a door.) GE also created a series of six-second videos of scientific experiments and encouraged consumers to share their own #6SecondScience videos, an effort that won an award at the Cannes Lions competition.

Try off-the-wall creativity. Does a snowball have a chance in a simulated hell? What if it was enclosed in a vessel made from the same material used in GE jet engines? To find out, GE encased a snowball in such a vessel and poured 2,000-degree molten steel over it. The snowball survived intact. Other topics were "catching lightning in a bottle" and "talking to a wall." A competition looked for the next idiom to test.

Employ vivid technologies. GE created stories with virtual-reality impact. The first followed an underwater submersible that mimics a GE subsea technology for discovering and collecting oil and gas deposits in the ocean. The underwater experience was simulated by having viewers wear Oculus Rift virtual-reality headsets while sitting in vibrating chairs.

Rely on humor. The geek world is celebrated by a character named Owen, who in an ad series describes to friends and family his new job at GE writing programs to help trains, planes and hospitals run better. They don't get it. In one ad, a family member tries to clarify: "So you are going to run a train?" In another, Owen's serious announcement is overshadowed by his friend's giddy excitement over making a new app for his hot gaming firm that can draw hats atop pictures of cats. The stories, intended to showcase GE's growing role in the digital industrial world, work because of their honest and funny portrayal of a geek/ not cool reality. The self-deprecating humor is worth sharing. And the geeks of the world get it: Owen, a continuing symbol of the new GE, is associated with an eight-fold increase in job applicants.

GE's efforts show how stories can adapt strategic messages to the social media age: Have clear communication objectives. Know your audiences. Be creative. Develop multiple approaches, and try the best of them. Tailor content to the medium; don't force it. Don't compromise on execution. And believe in storytelling that will interest and involve. Facts alone neither communicate nor persuade.

Creating Effective Signature Stories

What makes an effective signature story—one that connects, communicates and changes behavior in some way? We can look at some role models and observe their characteristics. We can examine research on stories. We can look at our own experience with stories. The results will be a long list of characteristics, some of which appear more often than others.

But high numbers of checkmarks on the list don't necessarily make a story more powerful. It just doesn't work that way. In fact, too many elements from the list can make a story ponderous and reduce the audience involvement that comes from imagining what's missing. A story's power depends instead on its context, objectives and audience, as well as the media involved. In each case, a different subset of the characteristics list will be employed. Instead of seeking as many desirable story characteristics as possible, aim for a few that "pop"—that gain your attention and involvement.

How the story characteristics interact and flow is also crucial. I once tried to figure out what makes a TV commercial effective by examining 100 characteristics—ranging from music to humor to whether the ad contained an animal. Ultimately, the effort failed because it was the total effect that mattered, not the sum of characteristics. Then we looked at pairs of similar ads that had very different levels of effectiveness.[2] Two commercials about fighting dandruff, for example, were identical (including the script) except for one thing—who was doing the talking. In the more effective ad, a smiling wife was delivering the "You have dandruff" message to her husband. In the less effective ad, the husband was delivering the same lines but came off as judgmental; the ad was thus irritating. The lesson: The impact of an ad or a story will be based on its total impression and flow, not on the sum of its parts.

Be Intriguing, Authentic and Involving, and Have a Strategic Message

Although the total impression is vital, it is still important to know the traits that are associated with successful signature stories and have been tested in research studies. These can help an organization evaluate and polish its stories. Several questions—all based on the definition of a signature story—can start the evaluation:

Is it a story? It should have a narrative with a beginning that captures your interest (the Blendtec iPod challenge from Chapter 2, for example), a middle that creates interest (the blending test itself) and a resolution ("Yes, it blends!") even if it is not told in that order. If it is a stand-alone set of facts or features, it will not qualify.

Is it intriguing? Does it grab your attention? Is it thought-provoking, novel, informative, inspiring, exceptionally relevant, humorous and/ or awe-creating? If it does not score highly on one or more of these dimensions, it will not gain attention and is thus not a good candidate for a signature story. The Skype story from Chapter 2, about the two girls who bonded though Skype, certainly qualifies along most of those dimensions.

Is it authentic? Do the settings, characters and challenges feel real? Or is the story likely to be perceived as phony, contrived or a transparent selling effort? Is there substance behind the story and its message? The Nordstrom story, in which an employee took back two used tires, illustrates employee empowerment, supported by policies that are visible to employees and even to shoppers.

A story can be fictional, as noted in Chapter 1. Indeed, a story that is clearly fictional may lead to a reduction in counter-arguing.[3] A danger is to come too close to a selling effort. There was a set of stories by a hotel chain around the value of fast check-out, and how guests used the saved time to visit local sites for interesting and exciting experiences. It did not do well perhaps because it came across as contrived and selling-focused.

Is it involving? Does it draw people in? Does it make you care? Knorr's #LoveAtFirstTaste experiment from Chapter 3 immediately had audiences wondering what would happen when two people who had never met were asked to feed each other. Does a story stimulate a cognitive response, such as a belief change, or an emotional response, such as feelings of warmth or awe? Will it cause the viewer to take action—maybe by passing along the story to others? A weak, shallow signature story is likely to result in a passive audience.

Charitable service organizations often have dozens of potentially compelling stories about those who receive their help. If told superficially, these stories will fail to capture the personality and emotion of the people involved. But when told thoughtfully through pictures and text, such stories have far-reaching, positive effects. Consider the charity: water story from Chapter 1, in which we get to know Natalia, who at age 15 became the president of her Mozambique village's water committee. It showed vividly how charity: water changed villagers' lives for the better.

Does it have a strategic message? The story should have a message that is strategically important to the organization, the brand, the customer relationship and/or the business strategy. Evaluate the message for its potential impact over time: How important is it? Is it central or just peripheral? Does it clarify or enhance a point of strength and/or neutralize a point of weakness? Will it endure or will it fade? Is it supported by visible and credible substance and honesty? And, finally, will it help fuel growth in key success measures like sales, profits and market position?

How do you create intriguing, authentic and involving stories? The GE case offers some suggestions. A story can involve technological breakthroughs, personal connections, brand heritage, audience interests, user-generated material, novel and vivid approaches, and humor. Again, effectiveness does not come from checking boxes but rather from the total effect. Still, it is useful to have an intriguing and absorbing plot, to consider the use of humor and to have an effective presentation.

An Intriguing, Absorbing Plot

The plot is the heart of the story. It needs to both grab and keep attention. That task will be aided if the story has these qualities:

Empathy for its characters. Characters are almost always central to a story. A good story brings its characters alive with interesting traits and enough detail so the audience gets to know and care about them. The story should generate real empathy for the characters, their challenges and their emotions. Remember Utari, the Indian mother celebrating her son's fifth birthday in the Lifebuoy video from Chapter 5? Viewers can sense her joy. In the L.L. Bean story from Chapter 1, we can visualize Leon Bean sitting in a duck blind or tying fish lures and sense his passion for outdoor life.

A meaningful challenge or obstacle. The challenge should be real and worthwhile, and should be overcome by the story hero. If a customer has only the problem of getting clothes clean and fresh, the challenge will appear too familiar, commercial and mundane. Who cares and who listens? But if a story is set in rural Mexico where there can be water shortages that affect people's lives, there is a meaningful challenge to which people can relate. When the Downy brand responds with Downy Single Rinse, a product that works with much less than the usual amount of water, the story gets traction.

Conflict and tension. These create emotional involvement, enhance memorability and make people care. In Knorr's #LoveAtFirstTaste experiment, when two strangers meet for a foodie date and must feed each other, we can sense the awkwardness and tension. On a more serious note, we can see conflict and tension in the IBM story from Chapter 7, when Lou Gerstner faced the stark choice between breaking up IBM or becoming a unified systems firm. Signature stories will usually benefit if there is a moment of tension or conflict and a reason to care about how it is resolved.

A surprise. Stories benefit from something that violates expectations. Surprise was in the air in the U.S. School of Music ad from Chapter 4, which showed a man sitting down to play the piano at a festive party and then becoming an artistic and social success. No one saw it coming! The same can be said of each MasterCard "Priceless Surprise" event described in Chapter 7. And in the Red Bull story from Chapter 3, audiences gasp when Felix Baumgartner steps off a platform more than 24 miles in the sky for his famous jump. Such moments generate a "Can you believe it?" reaction that motivates audiences to talk about an event and to pass along the story to others.

An emotional connection. These connections can bring great impact because they enhance other aspects of the story—including its ability to intrigue and to involve. They also provide rewards for attending to the story. Recall the emotion felt in the Always "like a girl" video from Chapter 3, when three young girls gave powerful meaning to what it was like to "run like a girl." It went viral because it provided all the rewards of sharing. By passing along the video to others, a viewer could show his or her empathy and feel good about sharing something so interesting, novel and touching.

In a study to find which stories made the "most e-mailed" lists, 7,000 articles from The New York Times were coded for their emotional content and whether that content was mild or intense.[4] Controlling for other variables—like the author's fame, the article's placement in the newspaper, or how informative it was—the study found that intense emotional response was a substantial predictor of an article's ability to stimulate a reader to share it by e-mail. When stories were rated very highly in creating awe (a rare treatment cures a patient, for example), anger (Wall Street pays hefty bonuses) or anxiety (home prices are far from bottoming), they were about one-third more likely to be e-mailed. The intensity of the emotion mattered more than the emotion type.

Relevance to the audience. Emotional moments can be magical in stories, but in many b-to-b contexts, a brand application's relevance in problem-solving can matter more. Recall from Chapter 1 the IBM Watson Health story, which showed the power of IBM's Watson in helping hospitals deliver personalized health care. The stories were intriguing and involving (and certainly authentic) because they were so relevant—the audience members are facing identical challenges and searching for solutions like the one presented.

Relevance can spring from stories that are simply interesting, without a lot of tension or emotion. GE took people on a first-hand tour of a test site near the North Pole. Maersk, the shipping firm, showed stories of docking the largest container ship in the port of Haifa, Israel. In this case, the stories' hero was an extraordinary ship.

An understandable message or theme. A story should offer a message that audience members can deduce for themselves. But don't make the message so subtle that people must struggle to get the point—an effort they are unlikely to make. They should not be left asking "So what?" but instead should be able to figure it out. In the Nordstrom story, the audience can understand that Nordstrom employees are empowered to make decisions and are concerned first about customers.

Links to the brand. If the brand is overshadowed by the plot or characters, a story will have less strategic value. There is no such issue when the brand is baked into the story, either as its hero or in another major role. The Blendtec, Nordstrom and Barclays stories are examples. But in some cases, the most powerful stories have no role for the brand. What to do then? Some possibilities, as discussed in Chapter 3, include using a founder story, having the story reflect the passion of the customer base, having the supporting programs carry the brand name and prominently displaying the brand as the story sponsor.

Humor

Humor is a powerful aspect of stories when it works and is on-message. Just think of how Abraham Lincoln used it so effectively.

Humor rewards the audience by entertaining. As such, it attracts and maintains attention. Exceptional humor will be shared—and can even go viral. People may pass along stories as a favor to their friends, or to express themselves as connoisseurs of worthwhile material. A humorous item can deliver both motivations.

Recall the Blendtec videos, in which Tom Dickson delivers a tough-in-cheek "scientific experiment" to see how his blender tackles various hard objects. The videos certainly have a "Can you believe it?" appeal. But much of their value comes from humor: Dickson's delivery and the exaggerated tension are both very funny. People look forward to the next version even though the "surprise" is baked into the story. The audience is in on a continuing inside joke.

In other cases, humor enhance communication by reducing counter-arguing and even defensive anger. Recall the discussion of how a story can divert people from counter-arguing by focusing attention on the story, thereby allowing the strategic message to slip through without being challenged. Humor accentuates the distraction and makes counter-arguing even less likely.

The use of humor has a risk: It can so dominate a message that the link with the brand is lost. But this risk is reduced if the brand can be built into the story, as in the Blendtec and the Coca-Cola "Happiness Machine" videos. In the Coke example, the familiar red soda dispenser is the story's hero and provides a link with the brand.

The Presentation

A great presentation cannot save a weak story, but an inferior presentation can damage a good one. The keys are what you say and how you present it.

The process can benefit greatly from professional guidance. The Lifebuoy videos, for example, would not have gone viral without outstanding creative craftsmanship. Top talent was needed to maximize the stories' suspense, surprise and emotion.

As with story content, presentation quality has no exact checklist. But we know that creating a visual image helps. It enhances memory and impact, makes it more likely that the content will be processed holistically and accentuates the effect of the story's positive elements.[5]

Visual images don't come from pictures and video alone. They also come from a detailed description of the story context, the personality of the characters, why they were doing what they were doing, and so on. All draw the audience into the scene. But the level of detail needs to be managed; too much can make a story ponderous. "More is better" is not the rule.

The use of video and related technologies, now increasingly accessible, can also make the story more intriguing, more involving, more authentic, more vivid and more memorable. All these techniques should be on the table:

Live streaming. In the Red Bull example from Chapter 3, live streaming of Felix Baumgartner's jump provided a level of interest and involvement not possible after the fact. Compare seeing a live basketball game with watching a taped replay when you already know the final score. Chevrolet has used live streaming to leverage events: The Chevrolet Bolt was launched at CES, the global consumer electronics trade show, via a 25-minute livestream clip on Facebook; Mary Barra, the CEO of General Motors, took part in the presentation. Some 25,000 viewers joined in, orders of magnitude more than the actual attendance at the event. Chevrolet also live-streamed a scavenger-hunt-themed race in Jakarta, Indonesia, for the introduction of the Chevrolet Trax.[6]

360-degree video. Samasource, a not-for-profit firm that trains tech workers in developing countries and matches them to high-tech projects, used this technique to create a four-minute video featuring a Samasource instructor who trains young people in Nairobi, Kenya, and two Samasource workers making a better life for themselves and their families.[7] The 360-degree view lets the audience get a full picture of living and working conditions, a qualitatively different experience than offered by a conventional video.

Augmented reality (AR). This technology adds images of people, animals, symbols or structures to what you are otherwise seeing. The most spectacular AR project has been Pokémon Go, in which people search their surroundings for Pokémon characters they can capture as they pop up before their eyes. It took just 19 days to achieve 50 million downloads of the game. Within a year, the number was 750 million, of which 50 million were active in an average month.[8] Many of these enthusiasts have their own Pokémon Go stories to share.

At a bus shelter in London, Pepsi altered the glass windows so those inside could see images of the approach of a lion, a person floating through the air and much more. A video recorded people's reactions, both during the experience and after they learned what was happening. This promotion story resulted in over $60 million in sales enhancement.[9]

Virtual reality (VR). In this immersive experience, the viewer is placed into scenes independent of his or her surroundings. A neuroscience study involving 150 respondents showed that a VR experience elicited 27 percent higher emotional engagement than one in a 2-D format. And the VR viewers stayed emotionally engaged for a 34 percent longer period.[10]

VR is particularly good at simulating travel experiences. A Chevrolet Colorado promotion in Thailand allowed viewers to experience an off-road driving adventure through the New Zealand countryside. The travel brand Expedia created VR "Dream Adventures" to bring the world to young patients at St. Jude Children's Research Hospital in Memphis, Tennessee. It offered wonderful therapy—an "out of the hospital" experience inside the hospital, and the story that went with it.[11]

Through VR, you can even travel to Mars. Lockheed Martin supported its education program with the Mars Experience Bus, replacing the windows of a school bus with glass allowing a VR scene of a Mars landscape to unfold outside. The resulting story garnered more than three million video views in its launch month.[12]

Much less complex was the "Happy Goggles" promotion by McDonald's in Sweden. In it, a VR viewer made from a Happy Meal box was tied to Sportlov, a Swedish recreational holiday. When participants put on the goggles, they could enter a ski-themed VR game called "Slope Stars."

Challenge: Crafting the Story and Getting It Right

A story works if it works—if it is right. Simply having a story is not a strategy. The story and its presentation should have home-run potential, then must be refined so they achieve it. Four story dimensions summarize the challenge.

First is content. The story needs the potential to intrigue and involve, and must be authentic. Look for story contexts that produce that impact.

As noted in Chapter 5, organizations benefit from having a higher purpose because the resulting stories usually have great content. A higher-purpose story like the Lifebuoy "Help a Child Reach 5" handwashing program is inspiring, engenders strong emotional response, creates vivid characters, has thought-provoking content and is dramatically authentic. No set of advertisements about a soap product alone is going to go viral and get 44 million hits like the three Lifebuoy videos did.

Second, as noted earlier in this chapter, stories shouldn't depend on a full, long checklist of desirable attributes. Instead, look for stories that stand out because they spike in maybe just a few of those elements. The story of Molson's mountain hockey rink has a "Can you believe it?" appeal. The Blendtec videos are so novel and funny that audiences want to share them. Going "over the top" in this way produces stories that can entertain, inform and create emotion.

Third, the story should click on many levels. It should have a strong beginning and end. It should have great timing, pacing, fit and flow. The length, context, emotion, tension and level of detail should feel right. Each story must reach the audience in its own way. But it's not easy. Look at the work of some good storytellers and see how their stories click. Those who have a good feel for storytelling know how to adjust their style for story type and context.

Fourth, because there is no exact formula for generating or evaluating signature stories, a "test and learn" approach makes sense, as illustrated by the GE case in this chapter. One thing is clear: When the right signature story is found, it should be valued, resourced and leveraged. It can be a significant asset.

YOUR PROFESSIONAL
SIGNATURE STORIES—
UNDERSTANDING YOURSELF

"Knowing yourself is the beginning of all wisdom."
—Aristotle

How I Got into Branding—the Back Story

n the mid-1980s, I was teaching business strategy from an external, marketing perspective and came to believe that executives were focusing too much on short-term financial results. They were basing decisions on a perceived need to increase sales and earnings to achieve performance targets. I concluded that this emphasis was damaging businesses and, indeed, the larger economy. The solution, as I saw it, was to elevate the long-term health of the business by building assets that would support future growth and profitability.

But what should my role be in this effort? What assets should I focus on? Where would I make a difference?

The answer turned out to be branding. Three factors guided me in this direction. First, I completed a study, published in 1989, in which some 248 executives were asked to name the assets and skills that gave their firms a sustainable competitive advantage.[1] Three of their top 10 responses were characteristics of their brands: quality reputation (which finished No. 1), name recognition (No. 3) and customer base (No. 10). Another top response, customer service (No. 2), was at least brand-related.

A second influence was my prior research and books on advertising, marketing and strategic marketing management. All provided a relevant background to study branding. The third factor was a new concept, brand equity, that was getting traction in business as firms sought to change their focus toward growing the size and loyalty of the customer base and away from using cost-cutting and brand-damaging price promotions.

With this analysis in place, I somewhat grandiosely decided that my future role would be to help firms recognize the asset power of their brands. I would help them learn to create, build, leverage and manage these assets. I hoped to play a small part in the movement to change how firms perceived their brands and, indeed, their marketing and business strategies.

At last, I had a direction and was no longer drifting opportunistically through my research career. I started the journey by embarking with my Berkeley-Haas colleague Kevin Keller on brand-extension research; by working with another colleague, Bob Jacobson, to relate brand equity and stock return econometrically; and by writing a book, "Managing Brand Equity." And then one thing led to another ….

Creating Your Professional Signature Story

The story above is one example of a professional signature story. Such stories should have the main attributes of other signature stories:

They should be intriguing, authentic and involving. But they should also have two other qualities:

- They should be relevant to your past, present or future career.
- They should give you a professional direction, provide a motivating rationale and/or illuminate your relevant professional strengths or weaknesses.

A set of professional signature stories can address career questions that are sometimes hard to answer directly. All professional managers or executives—or those on the track to these positions—will find value in articulating these story sets and periodically reviewing and expanding them. With these stories, they can find ways to savor the past, maximize the present and plan for the future.

Some business leaders have packaged their signature stories into books that chronicle their lives in a textured narrative. Among the many leaders who have done this well are Marc Benioff (Salesforce. com), Andy Grove (Intel), Lou Gerstner (IBM), A.G. Lafley (Procter & Gamble), Richard Branson (Virgin), Tony Hsieh (Zappos), Howard Schultz (Starbucks), Peter Guber (Columbia Pictures Entertainment) and Jack Welch (General Electric).[2]

A professional signature story can arise from many different sources. Maybe it was an event in your professional life—a notable success or failure, for example. Or an opportunity to change directions. Or the way another leader in your organization accomplished something outstanding or handled a situation poorly. Or how an outside role model did something you wanted to emulate. Or how a chapter from your personal life influenced your career. An example introduced in Chapter 5 is how Blake Mycoskie, the TOMS founder, saw the need for shoes among children in Argentina when he traveled there.

As with brand or organizational signature stories, a single story may capture your identity, direction and strategy. But in most cases, a set of stories is needed to fill that wide role. In my case, the umbrella story of how I got into branding is elaborated by many supporting stories. For example, each of my research directions had an underlying motivation and was stimulated by an issue, article or person. My second book on branding, "Building Strong Brands," and my "brand identity model" were triggered by managers seeking practical tools for building and managing brands. All these stories and more are found in my life story, "From Fargo to the World of Brands, Third Edition."[3]

Professional signature stories have many roles and objectives. Here are four questions they can answer—the first three focusing on being introspective and understanding yourself, and the fourth on making yourself and your stories credible to others:

- Who am I professionally?
- What is the higher purpose in my work?
- Where am I going and how will I get there?
- How do I gain trust, credibility and connection?

The most relevant and powerful professional signature stories will usually play more than one of these roles—and often all four.

"Who Am I?" Stories

Professional signature stories can help identify fundamental dimensions of your work life. What is your professional role? Your contribution? Why are you doing what you are doing? What are your strengths? How have you leveraged them?

A professional signature story offers insight into values that you could jot down in a simple, self-descriptive list. Maybe you call yourself ethical, innovative, loyal and supportive of your colleagues. The story adds substance, texture and clarity to those values, with the potential to be vivid and memorable. Sometimes the story has a single defining moment, but often the story involves a journey. It may have to do with career choices, a mentor's guidance and/or lessons learned from successes or failures.

Career-choice stories. Why did you choose your career or join your organization? What motivated or inspired you? Is there a story that reflects your rationale—and your excitement about the decision?

Rich Lyons, the charismatic dean of the Berkeley-Haas School of Business, tells a story that explains his commitment to the school. He was an undergrad there when a professor of public policy noticed his performance in class and called him into her office and asked whether he would consider getting a Ph.D. and becoming a professor. This idea was completely new to him—way off his radar screen. But at her suggestion, he met with an economist on the faculty. From that point, the idea grew into a reality. Five years after graduating from Berkeley-Haas in 1982, he got his Ph.D. in economics from M.I.T. After six years as a professor of international finance at Columbia, he returned "home" to Berkeley-Haas as an award-winning teacher, an impactful researcher and, ultimately, an outstanding dean. He often tells this story to illustrate his attachment to his alma mater—and his appreciation for the fact that a world-class public university can inspire students who can't afford a private-school education to achieve amazing things.

The influence of a mentor. Recall from Chapter 5 the story set developed by the Charles Schwab financial firm in conjunction with CNN. In these emotionally powerful stories, 12 CNN anchors described "The Person Who Changed My Life."[4] Michaela Pereira's mentor, for example, gave her the confidence to enter television, and Ashleigh Banfield's mentor and role model, her mother, taught her to be resilient.

Another anchor, Erin Burnett, provided a story for the set that reflected on her drive and direction—and on the mentor who gave her a chance. Burnett was a young analyst at Goldman Sachs when she wrote a letter to Willow Bay, a former Estée Lauder model who earned an M.B.A. and became an anchor for CNN. Burnett explained how she had followed Bay's career path and wanted to join her staff. Bay, impressed with the initiative shown in the letter, interviewed and hired her. Bay and the executive producer of her show appeared on the story video to comment on that first impression, as well as on Burnett's talent and willingness to do any task. Burnett is now a star of CNN's programing—and it would not have happened without that letter.

Success/failure stories. Reflect on your success stories, or other enjoyable times in your career. Too often, they become lost in the jumble of daily life. Yet they can say much about your strengths and skills—and can thwart the temptation to view your life and job as boring and inconsequential. What were the successes about? What motivated your programs or initiatives? How were they developed and carried out? What worked and what didn't? What were the outcomes?

When he was CEO of Medtronic, the medical device firm, Bill George was observing an operation when a Medtronic balloon catheter failed during an operation. [5] He later found out that a Medtronic sales rep had observed several such cases and had reported them back to the home office. But such reports had to go through seven organizational units before they got to product designers who were insulated from users of the equipment. George committed to a 10-year program of making hospitals, doctors and patients central to the company's operations, starting with a process to link product designers with customers. The story supported the idea of customer-centered programs, but it also showed how George valued customers, valued first-hand contact with them, and dealt with issues as they arose.

Stories of success can demonstrate your accomplishments and breadth, perhaps illuminating talents you hadn't realized were there. Together, these "I can do that" moments show that your skills aren't as narrow as your current job might imply—and that you are capable of much more.

Failure stories can provide insights as well as learning opportunities. What was your most significant failure? How did it happen? What lessons did you learn from it? How did it make you a better professional? Was a personal weakness or involved? If so, how might that weakness be lessened, neutralized or removed? Such stories make the lessons more visible and more tangible.

Reflecting on your "Who am I?" signature stories can be healthy because they provide a realistic assessment of who you are as a person and where you are in your career. They also reduce a tendency to underplay your organizational role and achievements. Finally, these stories allow you to relive your experiences at some level, and to savor them. Without these stories, the savoring is all too short-lived.

Higher-Purpose Stories

All professionals will perform better, find their work more meaningful and be happier in general if they have one or more higher purposes in their professional lives. You want a reason to go to work and to be a positive-thinking colleague. Recall the story at the outset of Chapter 5, highlighting the difference between viewing oneself as working at a task, earning a wage or being a builder of a cathedral. What is your higher purpose? What personal goals, or those of your organization, give meaning to your professional life? And what stories provide clarity to that higher purpose?

The story of how a higher purpose emerged in your career can illuminate its motivation and the resulting commitment. For me, the higher purpose was a goal beyond publishing articles and books— namely, to encourage firms to step away from short-term thinking and to move toward asset-building. More specifically, it was to make the building and leveraging of brand assets a part, if not the driver, of how marketing is perceived and businesses are run. The story recounted at the outset of this chapter supports that commitment.

Consider Howard Schultz's higher-purpose story. Schultz took over Starbucks in 1987, when the chain had only a few stores. From the start, his core values included respect for all employees and a belief in a quality workplace. He wanted employees to find meaning in their working lives, whether they were baristas or members of the logistics team getting fresh coffee beans to the stores.[6] The first version of its mission statement had six principles—the first being to "provide a great work environment and treat each other with respect and dignity." Since then, the words have changed but not the sentiment. In part because of his commitment, Starbucks decided early on to offer health coverage and stock benefits to all employees, even part-timers.

A story about his father explains the depth of Schultz's commitment to treating employees with dignity. As a youngster, Howard watched his father get beaten down by the system even though he worked hard, sometimes with two jobs. He had to quit school to go to work, then would suffer from malaria contracted as a soldier in World War II. He never found a job with much of a future or even one that offered respect and meaning. In 1961, he would suffer a foot injury that meant extra costs with no health insurance and no income. Howard resolved that if he was ever able to make a difference, he would not leave others behind.

Another higher-purpose professional story, introduced in Chapter 1, is that of Marc Benioff, CEO of Salesforce.com. A retreat in India led Benioff to believe that a social purpose could be built into a business.[7] That belief resulted in Salesforce's 1-1-1 programs, whereby 1 percent of the firm's output, 1 percent of equity and 1 percent of employees' time are devoted to social programs. The story has provided inspiration and guidance to Benioff in his leadership role—not only of his firm but also of the high-tech community.

The Benioff story also involves employee initiative and leadership, providing a clear path for employees to create higher-purpose stories of their own. Sue Amar's story is an example. Early in the life of Salesforce. com, Amar, then a senior business analyst there, asked during an annual open forum what the firm was doing about the environment. Benioff replied by asking her to take six paid days off to figure it out. That challenge would become a turning point in her career. She came back with a plan for the firm to reduce its carbon footprint. She later helped form and lead the "Earth Council," an employee-run group that examined grass-roots changes within the company to address the climate crisis. But the story didn't end there. In its next chapter, she was assigned to a new role as the first sustainability manager at Salesforce, tasked with helping it establish an environmental mission statement and integrate policies supporting sustainable business practices. Her story thus provided a role-model signature story for other Salesforce employees.

"Where Am I Going?" Stories

Professional signature stories can help you create, refine and articulate a career path, with a set of goals and strategic priorities. And these stories can provide both short- and long-term guidance. At Salesforce, Sue Amar found not only a higher purpose but also a new career direction with a plan that evolved over time.

My set of signature stories helped guide my research, teaching and writing—and, eventually, my decision to join a brand consulting firm. It all stemmed from my choosing to help organizations build their brand assets. The result was systematic growth in my personal professional assets—particularly my books and articles, with the concepts and frameworks they contained. Much of my past work on ad hoc projects would become a foundation for my branding work and a synergistic source of strength and differentiation. Just as important, I came to understand that I was less productive and less happy doing ad hoc projects that didn't seem to go anywhere or have a lasting impact.

"Where am I going?" stories can involve useful general guidance rather than specific plans. In a 2005 commencement address at Stanford that would go viral, Steve Jobs offered several career-advice stories.[8] In one, he told of dropping out of college early because it was costing the life savings of his parents, who had adopted him only after promising his birth mother that he would get a college education. As a result, he stopped taking required courses and started sitting in on interesting ones while living an extremely austere life, which included sleeping on the floor in friends' rooms. One course, on calligraphy, seemed frivolous but would later influence fonts and visuals for the Mac computer and, ultimately, for much of the computer interface software we know today. The point of the story: Study broadly, because you can't predict what will become useful. Only later will you connect the dots.

Another story involves his departure from and ultimate return to Apple, the firm he co-founded in 1976. Pushed out of his operational role in 1985, he would soon leave the firm. He felt devastated and considered leaving Silicon Valley. But his love and passion for innovation in computer industry made him start over: He founded NeXT, a computer company with an agile operating system friendly to software developers. In 1996, Apple bought NeXT in part for the operating system and in part to get Jobs to come back. So, almost a dozen years after he first left, Jobs returned to restore Apple to its innovative ways. The point? Follow your heart and do what you love. If you don't find the path at first, keep looking. Don't settle.

Although general advice can be helpful, detailed plans can be a crucial part of a professional signature story. Where are you going and why? Who will join you on the journey? What is your destination and how will you get there? What are the landmarks along the way? If your story involves a career change, the details could include a new job profile, an M.B.A. program and interim goals. Any career story that offers detail and vision will evolve as new opportunities and obstacles arise. But without such a story, a career may wander aimlessly or, more likely, just stagnate.

A professional signature story that charts a career vision allows others to understand your goals, your strategy for reaching them, your will to succeed and the assets you bring. By knowing the story, your subordinates can better decide to follow you. Your peers can decide to join you. And those above you can decide whether to enable your vision to succeed. That was true for Zhang Ruimin, whose signature story provided a direction for him, his firm and many fellow employees who adapted his story for their own.

Zhang was promoted in 1984 to lead a then-struggling Chinese refrigerator manufacturer that would later be renamed Haier. After a customer brought in a faulty refrigerator, Zhang and the customer went through his entire inventory of 400 refrigerators looking for a replacement—only to find that nearly 20 percent were defective. A special moment had arrived: Zhang promptly had the 76 dud refrigerators lined up on the factory floor, gave employees sledgehammers and ordered the machines destroyed. A dramatic decision indeed.

Zhang's signature story led to a change in the firm's culture and strategy, with an ongoing commitment to quality that affected product development, operations, manufacturing and the evaluation of employees. The story would also change the way the brand was perceived by customers and dealers—as one that could deliver world-class quality under the leadership of a charismatic and innovative CEO. Haier would become a major Chinese success story with a global footprint, and Zhang would become a national hero and a renowned management innovator. His story remains a spiritual cornerstone of his leadership journey.

Signature Stories in Your Personal Life

Your signature stories can influence your career path even if they are not directly relevant to your professional role. And they certainly can play important roles in your personal life. They help define what makes you happy and what gives you meaning. Most personal signature stories involve your family, friends, traditions and activities–and perhaps your health or your ways of helping others. But they also can include memorable stories about role models or others who may have gained your respect and admiration.

Personal signature stories provide several benefits. They enhance memories, allowing you to savor special experiences. They show your values in action. Finally, by identifying relationships and activities that are healthy and productive, versus those that are dysfunctional, these stories help you prioritize your time and allocate resources.

Try this exercise: Look back on your last month or your last year: What experiences provided happiness or meaning in your life? What people do you remember most, and what interactions best represented your relationship with them? What actions exemplified your higher purpose or best instincts? What situations provided joy, relief, pride or admiration? Now use those insights to build a story that is intriguing, authentic and involving. Look for challenges, big or small, and emotional moments.

The exercise can be applied to your whole life. I wrote an autobiography that packaged hundreds of personal signature stories. It was a most rewarding effort, and I would recommend such an undertaking to anyone. In my case, the power of personal signature stories was exemplified by those involving my three daughters.

Even at a young age, my daughters—Jennifer, Jan and Jolyn—tended to relate to one another more than to me, and it was a struggle for me to establish a close relationship with each. The solution? One-on-one adventures with the label "special days." I would announce an upcoming special day for one daughter, which meant that she could look forward to a surprise event planned just for her. (And it's hard to turn down a surprise, isn't it?) For me, of course, the day would offer quality time with one of my children.

I still remember vividly that first special day, when Jennifer, then age 6, went for a hike with me in the Berkeley Hills; we discussed life and picked poppies. We had fun, though we learned later that picking poppies was against the law and still later that outdoorsy stuff wouldn't be Jennifer's thing for long. Eventually, our special days might involve a visit to a bookstore, with the adventure of selecting the right book—and with me gently manipulating the choice toward something "educational." One "lesson" was that if you buy something for someone (or at least Jennifer at the time), she likes you more. Kind of an economic principle.

These special days were sometimes very special. Jan was surprised to be taken to the airport for a trip to an Aaker family reunion at Child Lake in northern Minnesota. The reunion was at the cabin of my Uncle Bjarne, my all-time favorite person—the type who makes all things positive. We would canoe among the loons, walk the forest trails and hang out by the fireplace with the some of my 15 cousins. The trip offered memories galore, including Jan's delight at the airport when she learned she was going on the trip. For

Jolyn, one special day involved a helicopter ride over San Francisco Bay. Again, the memories were precious. There was the anticipation of boarding the helicopter, the actual takeoff and flight, and the chance to see Alcatraz from the air for a long time.

Indeed, these special-day stories have had a long life, though it is the overall umbrella story, the meta story, that is a large part of our family lore and has given meaning to my life.

Beyond the special days, of course, there were many meaningful moments that allowed me to grow closer to my daughters. Those occasions, too, have resulted in stories with rich detail. I remember calling Jennifer when she was in a low spot on a European summer trip and turning her discouragement into joy when I said I would meet her in London in a few days. (We ended up doing some significant shopping, seeing "Les Misérables" for the first time and taking a memorable road trip to Bath.) I remember spending time with Jan before her wedding, sharing memories and then walking her across the bridge for the ceremony. And I remember how, after following Jolyn's soccer career (some say too closely) through college, I wrote a story summarizing her journey in the sport—with all its challenges and rewards, the gift of playing at a high level, her interactions with teammates and coaches, and the emotions of winning and losing—but also describing what a ride it was for me.

One early parenting challenge was how to expose the children to great classical music. One partial solution was to attend "The Nutcracker" ballet. When the first two were 3 and 5, we started going to see it in San Francisco. Part of the deal was to get dressed up for the ballet and, once in the theater, to observe the dresses of others, picking out the best two or three. We have gone for each of the 40-plus years since—now with the kids of my kids. This "Nutcracker meta story" helps define our life together.

These signature stories and others, often stimulated by unforgettable emotional moments, bring alive the girls' personalities, values and relationships. But such stories also influence my own priorities, traditions and future activities because they help show what is important in life.

Signature Stories That Gain Trust, Credibility and Connection

A crucial communication task for any organizational leader is to motivate others—most notably one's employees, but sometimes customers, investors, suppliers and the public. To do so, a leader needs to build trust, earn credibility and create a connection with his or her audience, particularly when that audience is employees. Without that relationship, the leader won't be able to make the sale. The challenge is greater when a person is new to the organization or has lost credibility for some reason.

To develop trust, credibility and a connection, leaders first need to introduce themselves. And facts alone do not work. You can't say:

- I am a good person—honest, moral, empathetic, concerned with others and able to acknowledge mistakes.
- I am trustworthy; you can believe what I say.
- I am a talented person—smart, well-informed, creative and good with people.

Such simple assertions will be unconvincing—and an invitation to ridicule. But telling a personal story that implies the same assertions will be accepted. It is just a story, but it can build trust, credibility and liking.

Signature stories help define and support authentic leadership.[9] Two scholars did an exhaustive review of the literature around such leadership and concluded that two of its characteristics were clarity about self-knowledge (knowing yourself as you really are) and about self-concept (how you would describe yourself to others). Both are needed. They suggest that a good way to improve your ability to be an authentic leader is to introspectively create and clarify life stories, narratives about self-relevant events across time and their relationship to one another. In other words, identify and articulate your signature stories. Research suggests that the opinions and actions of one's followers are based on a judgment of authenticity. And that judgment, in turn, is based on the believability of the leader's signature stories and whether the stories match the leader's actions.[10]

A story about correcting a past misstep, for example, can help show your management style or emphasize a part of the culture that is particularly important to you. It may also offer a way to introduce some self-deprecating humor. The story will show that you recognize mistakes, learn from them and aren't deadly serious about everything. That makes people want to listen. By contrast, consider a leader who lectures with an efficient PowerPoint presentation about culture or strategy—but offers only concepts and facts, with nothing personal. The response would likely be boredom, skepticism ("I've heard that before") and, ultimately, a lack of buy-in—or maybe even disrespect.

Or the story could be about a moment of aspiration, when an event triggered a personal professional purpose. Remember Zhang Ruimin's decision to destroy the defective appliances? It reflected his passion for quality and the goal for his firm to be a major player in the appliance scene in China. Had he simply asserted that objective, he wouldn't have connected with his employees. But the story added the CEO's personal passion and commitment to the words.

As noted in the previous chapter, humorous stories can be powerful partly because they entertain and partly because they inhibit counter-arguing. In a personal context, humor is particularly useful because it builds relationships and creates a more pleasant, even fun, work experience. You want to work with people who have a sense of humor, particularly of the self-deprecating variety. You want to feel that it's O.K. to lighten up.

In business settings, humor can also defuse tension, thus enhancing productivity. Important meetings can easily become acrimonious and stressful. A humorous story can dissolve the anxiety in the room, making others feel more relaxed and less uptight. The result is more creativity and risk-taking in expressing ideas.

When you need to point out the faults of a decision, a program or a person, humor offers additional benefits. Laughter can replace arguing and anger, bringing introspection and acceptance. Recall from Chapter 6 what Budd Cheit, who twice served as dean of the Berkeley-Haas School of Business, had to say about salaries. He observed that economists understood why they received higher pay than English professors but could not understand why finance professors earned more than them. He made a delicate point that, without humor, could have raised resentment. Instead of making others defensive, humor can show a side of you that is disarmingly likable.

Challenge: Just Doing It

Stories seldom happen by themselves. They require effort. Review your career, noting your achievements as well as other moments that led to a surge of confidence, a sense of pride or joy, or a change in career direction. Create a story bank—an organized compilation of these stories. Place them in something as simple as a small set of folders.

Then review, revise and reprioritize them periodically. When new stories surface, add them to the bank.

Use these stories to learn about yourself (Who am I?), the meaning in your professional life (What is my higher purpose?), your career trajectory (Where am I going?) and your credibility (How can it be enhanced?). Then use them to address basic professional issues that are affecting your job performance and career. Stories should become the springboard to reflection on the direction of your professional life.

You should also use stories to create relationships and communicate yourself to others. Be careful of offending or sending the wrong message, but don't be too cautious, either. Remember the power of stories. They are attended to, processed and remembered far more than a presentation of facts—and they can say so much about you.

Epilogue

12 TAKEAWAYS

"It ain't over till its over."
—Yogi Berra, baseball legend

What do you think are the dozen top takeaways from this book? Here are my choices:

Stories are powerful. Stories are amazingly more impactful than facts—significantly better at gaining attention, getting processed, being remembered, persuading, inspiring and stimulating action.

Signature stories take stories to the next level. A signature story is an intriguing, authentic and involving narrative that includes a strategic message. It is not a set of facts but can motivate facts that support the message.

Sets of signature stories can multiply the effect. Multiple stories from different perspectives can add depth and breadth to the strategic message, and give it freshness and energy.

Signature stories elevate a brand. They create visibility and energy, two key brand characteristics. Visibility comes from the stories' ability to gain attention and break through the media clutter. Energy springs from that visibility and the way the story involves the audience.

Signature stories persuade without lecturing. Instead, they allow audience members to deduce the message by themselves—and to remember it. And the stories distract from counter-arguing.

Higher-purpose signature stories inspire employees and customers. A higher purpose can give employees a new sense of pride in their work, and can motivate customers to support a brand because they share its values. The Lifebuoy "Help a Child Reach 5" program, for example, creates emotional involvement—and helps save lives.

Signature stories can help change the conversation when a brand is in crisis. When a brand trust crisis occurs perhaps precipitated by a product or service blunder or a news event, part of the response strategy can be to generate a new conversation around a brand program communicated in story form. The Barclays signature stories, about employee programs that teach people how to adapt to the digital world, helped turn around perceptions of a troubled brand.

Signature stories are vehicles to promote the strategic message. In the quest to find the most intriguing, involving story, the strategic message should never be lost. The goal is not just to find or create great stories. It's also to keep the message front and center over time.

Signature stories have all kinds of heroes. Often, they are employees or customers. But the hero can also be a product or service itself—or an organization program, a founder, a revitalization strategy, a growth strategy, a brand, a brand endorser or a supplier.

Signature stories "pop" in a few dimensions. Beyond being intriguing, authentic and involving, effective signature stories follow no long or exact checklist. But they benefit from having characters with whom we can empathize, a meaningful challenge, an emotional connection, high relevance (especially in b-to-b settings) and a professional presentation. In addition, humor helps them gain attention and distract from counter-arguing.

Signature stories can be personal. A personal professional signature story helps you understand yourself, identify your higher purpose, chart your future course and gain credibility.

An organization must be story-friendly. Your organization needs people, structures, processes and a culture that enable it to identify and evaluate story candidates, turn the best stories into professional presentations and, finally, expose them to target audiences.

About the Author

David Aaker, the Vice-Chairman of Prophet (a global brand and strategy consultancy) and Professor Emeritus of Marketing Strategy at the Berkeley-Haas School of Business, is the winner of four career awards for contributions to the science of marketing (Paul D. Converse Award), marketing strategy (Vijay Mahajan Award), the theory and practice of marketing (Buck  Weaver Award), and outstanding contributions to the field of marketing (the NYAMA Marketing Hall of Fame). He has published more than one hundred articles and seventeen books that have sold well over one million copies and been translated into eighteen languages. They include *Managing Brand Equity, Building Strong Brands, Brand Leadership* (co-authored with Erich Joachimsthaler) *Brand Portfolio Strategy, From Fargo to the World of Brands, 3rd edition, Spanning Silos, Strategic Market Management 10th edition, Brand Relevance: Making Competitors Irrelevant* which was named to three best book lists for 2011, *Three Threats to Brand Relevance,* and *Aaker on Branding.* Named as one of the top five most important marketing/business gurus in 2007, Professor Aaker has won awards for the best article in the California Management Review and (twice) in the Journal of Marketing. A recognized authority on brand strategy, he has been an active consultant and speaker throughout the world. A columnist for AMA's Marketing News and Germany's absatzwirtschaft, he regularly blogs at davidaaker.com and Linkedin. He is at twitter.com/davidaaker. An avid biker and struggling golfer, he lives in Orinda California.

ENDNOTES

Chapter 1

1   Phytel Helps Orlando Health Build a Clinically Integrated Network for a Healthier Community," IBM.com, 2016.

2   Peter Guber, "Tell to Win," New York: Crown Publishing, 2011, pp. 10-13.

3   Sellers-Easton Media, for example, was founded by top Fortune writers.

4   See Essential.com for a more detailed version of the story and the firm. A full-page ad in The Wall Street Journal presents the story and the principles, May 30, 2017, p. A5.

5   Marc Benioff and Carly Adler, "Behind the Cloud," San Francisco: Jossey-Bass, 2009.

6   Guber, op. cit., pp. 120-121.

Chapter 2

1   The campaign was at 135 million views when an analysis named it the top viral campaign in 2010. Now at 300 million views, it is very likely more solidly in the No. 1 position. Michael Learmonth, "The Top 10 Viral Ads of All Time," Advertising Age, September 2, 2010.

2   Alan Siegel, "Ad Meter 50 for 50th: Ranking the 50 Best Super Bowl Commercials Ever," USA Today, January 21, 2016.

3   Max Slonim, Charles Schwab Financial Services, "The Person Who Changed My Life," WARC, 2017.

4   charitywater.org/about/Scott-Harrison-story, 2017.

5   Prophet.com, Our Work, Case Studies, 2017.

6   Megan Willett, "Chinese Tourists Are Flooding Into the U.S. Thanks to a New Visa Rule," businessinsider.com, January 21, 2015.

Chapter 3

1   Matt Prentis, "Knorr: #LoveAtFirstTaste," WARC, 2016.

2   John Gerzema and Ed Lebar, "The Brand Bubble," San Francisco: Jossey-Bass, 2008, Chapter 2.

3   John Gerzema, personal conversation, July 2016.

4   Natalie Mizik and Robert Jacobson, "The Financial Value Impact of Perceptual Brand Attributes," Journal of Marketing Research, February 2008.

5   An excellent book that analyzes how to gain both short-term and extended attention is "Captivology: The Science of Capturing People's Attention," by Ben Parr. New York: HarperCollins Publishing, 2015.

6   Robert East, Jenni Romaniuk, Rahul Chawdhary and Mark Uncles, "The Impact of Word of Mouth on Intention to Purchase Currently Used and Other Brands," International Journal of Market Research, 59 (3),2017.

7   Elihu Katz and Paul F. Lazarsfeld, "Personal Influence," Glencoe, Illinois: The Free Press, 1955.

8   Ernest Dichter, "How Word-of-Mouth Advertising Works," Harvard Business Review, November-December 1966, pp. 147-166.

9   For a good overview of word-of-mouth research, see "Contagious: Why Things Catch On," by Jonah Berger. New York: Simon & Schuster, 2013.

Chapter 4

1   Paul Johnson, "A History of the American People," New York: Harper Collins, 1997.

2   Herb Simon's concept of bounded rationality can be applied.

3   Russell Haley and Allan Baldinger, The ARF Copy Research Validity Project, Journal of Advertising Research, April/May 1991, pp. 11-32; Andrew Mitchell and Jerry Olson, "Are Product Attribute Beliefs the Only Mediator of Advertising Effects on Brand Attitude?" Journal of Marketing Research, 18 (3), August 1981, pp. 318-332.

4   John P. Murry, John L. Lastovicka, Surendra Singh, "Feeling and Liking Responses to Television Programs," Journal of Consumer Research, March 1992, pp. 441-451.

5   Ton Van Laer, Ko de Ruyter, Luca M. Visconti and Martin Wetzels, "The Extended Transportation-Imagery Model: A Meta-Analysis of the Antecedents and Consequences of Consumers' Narrative Transportation," Journal of Consumer Research, February 2014, p. 2.

6   Deborah Small, George Loewenstein and Paul Slovic (2007), "Sympathy and Callousness: The Impact of Deliberative Thought on Donations to Identifiable and Statistical Victims," Organizational Behavior and Human Decision Processes, 102 (2), pp. 143-153.

7   Penelope Green, "He Takes Stuff Seriously: At Home With Joshua Glenn," nytimes.com, July 11, 2012.

8   Ton Van Laer et. al. op. cit. pp. 797-817.

9   Melanie C. Green and Timothy C. Brock, "The Role of Transportation in the Persuasiveness of Public Narratives," Journal of Personality and Social Psychology, 79 (5), 2000, pp. 701-721.

10   In a review of 225 studies, active learning was shown to be significantly more effective than passive learning in school settings. S. Freeman, S.L. Eddy, M. McDonough, M.K. Smith, N. Okoroafor, H. Jordt and M.P. Wenderoth, "Active Learning Increases Student Performance in Science, Engineering and Mathematics," Proceedings of the National Academy of Sciences, June 2014, pp. 8410-8415.

11   Melanie C. Green, "Narratives and Cancer Communication," Journal of Communication, August 2006, pp. S163-S183.

12   See Robert A. Burton, "On Being Certain," New York: St. Martin's Griffin, 2008.

13   Leon Festinger, Henry W. Riecken and Stanley Schachter, "When Prophecy Fails: A Social and Psychological Study of a Modern Group That Predicted the Destruction of the World," New York: Harper-Torchbooks, 1956.

14   Chip Heath and Dan Heath, "Made to Stick: Why Some Ideas Survive and Others Die," New York: Random House, 2007, pp. 42-244.

15   A.C. Graesser, N.L. Hoffman and L.F. Clark, "Structural Components of Reading Time," Journal of Verbal Learning and Verbal Behavior, 19 (2), April 1980, pp. 135-151.

16   Larry Cahill and James L. McGaugh, "A Novel Demonstration of Enhanced Memory Associated with Emotional Arousal," Consciousness and Cognition, 4 (4), December 1994, pp. 410-421.

17   Denise Davidson and Sandra B. Vanegas, "The Role of Emotion on the Recall of Central and Peripheral Information From Script-Based Text," Cognition and Emotion, 29 (1), 2015, pp. 76-94; Cara Laney, Hannah V. Campbell, Friderike Heuer, Daniel Reisberg, "Memory for Thematically Arousing Events," Memory & Cognition, 32 (7), 2004, pp. 1149-1159.

18   For a discussion of the power of triggers in promoting word-of-mouth communication, see Jonah Berger, "Contagious: Why Things Catch On," New York: Simon & Schuster, 2016.

Chapter 5

1   Leon Kaye, "Unilever Handwashing Campaign Goes Beyond CSR and Saves Lives," triplepundit.com, April 22, 2015.

2   Marc Benioff, "Behind the Cloud," San Francisco: Jossey-Bass, 2009, p. 147.

Chapter 6

1   Tom Roach, "Barclays: Purpose Pays," WARC, 2016.

2   Millward Brown Tracking, Roach op. cit., Figure 3.

3   Edelman Financial Trust Barometer 2014 had banks and the financial sector as the least-trusted industry in both 2013 and 2014, Roach op. cit., Figure 2.

4   "Banking on Change: Breaking the Barriers to Financial Inclusion," Barclays.com, 2017

5   Roach, op. cit.

6   Howard Schultz, "Pour Your Heart Into It," New York: Hyperion, 1997, Chapter 3.

7   Starbucks.com, 2017

Chapter 7

1   "Dispensing Happiness: How Coke Harnesses Videos to Spread Happiness," Stanford Graduate School of Business, Case M-335, June 9, 2010.

2   "Priceless Surprises," Reggie Awards, ANA.net, April 20, 2016.

3   According to BrandJapan-2017, an annual survey by Nikkei BP Consulting Inc. of 1,000 brands in the Japanese market.

4   Ariel Conant, "The Incredible Story of Marin Minamiya," YouthPost, yp.scmp.com, May 1, 2016.

5   Conant, op. cit.

6   Personal communication with John Gerzema, November 2016.

7   "Tequila Don Julio—Make Your Move," Reggie Awards, ANA.net, April 15, 2015.

8   Louis V. Gerstner Jr., "Who Says Elephants Can't Dance?" New York: Harper Business, 2002.

9   Brad Stone, "The Everything Store: Jeff Bezos and the Age of Amazon," New York: Back Bay Books, 2013.

Chapter 8

1   For more, see "GE: Reinventing Storytelling for Business-to-Business," ANA.net, Marketing Knowledge Center, 2016; Linda Boff, "Marketing

Transformation at GE: Storytelling and Business Results," YouTube, Columbia Business School, 2016.

2   ² "Causes of Irritation in Advertising?" (with Donald B. Bruzzone), Journal of Marketing, Spring 1985, pp. 47-57.

3   M C. Green, J. Garst and T.C. Brock, "The Power of Fiction: Determinants and Boundaries," in L.J. Shrum (ed.) "The Psychology of Entertainment Media: Blurring the Lines Between Entertainment and Persuasion," Mahwah, N.J.: Lawrence Erlbaum, pp. 161-176.

4   Jonah Berger and Katherine Milkman, "What Makes Online Content Viral?," Journal of Marketing Research, April 2012, 49 (2), pp. 192-205.

5   Rashmi Adaval and Robert S. Wyer Jr., "The Role of Narratives in Consumer Information Processing," Journal of Consumer Psychology, 1998, 7 (3), pp. 207-245.

6   Low Lai Chow, "General Motors Taps Augmented Reality, Live Streaming for Better Customer experience," WARC, September 2016.

7   "Why Work Matters," Nairobi 360 Degrees, Samasource.org/impact, April 2017.

8   Craig Smith, "80+ Incredible Pokémon Go Statistics and Facts," expandedramblings.com, DMR Statistics, June 2017.

9   WARC Trends, Toolkit 2017, "How Brands Can Use Virtual and Augmented Reality," WARC, 2017.

10   Jeff Berman, "YuMe, Nielsen: VR Has Potential for Marketers, but Also Presents New Challenges," MESA M&E Connections, November 10, 2016.

11   WARC Trends, op. cit.

12   WARC Trends, op. cit.

Chapter 9

1   David Aaker, "Managing Assets and Skills: The Key to a Sustainable Competitive Advantage," California Management Review, 31 (2), January 1, 1989, pp. 91-106.

2   Marc Benioff, "Beyond the Cloud," San Francisco: Jossey-Bass, 2009; Andrew S. Grove, "Only the Paranoid Survive," New York: Crown Business, 1999; Louis V. Gerstner Jr., "Who Says Elephants Can't Dance?," New York: HarperBusiness, 2003; A.G. Lafley & Ram Charan, "The Game-Changer," New York: Crown Business, 2008; Richard Branson, "Losing My Virginity," London: Virgin Books, 2007; Tony Hsieh, "Delivering Happiness," New York: Grand Central Publishing, 2013; Howard Schultz, "Pour Your Heart Into It," New York: Hyperion, 1997; Peter Guber, "Tell to Win," New York: Crown Business, 2011; Jack Welch and John Byrne, "Jack: Straight From the Gut," New York: Warner Business Books, 2001.

3   David Aaker, "From Fargo to the World of Brands," Tucson, Ariz.: Wheatmark Books, 2016.

4   Max Slonim, Charles Schwab Financial Services: "The Person Who Changed My Life," WARC, 2017.

5   Rick Levine, Christopher Locke, Doc Searls, David Weinberger, "The Clue Train Manifesto," Cambridge, Mass.: Perseus Books, 2000, p.100.

6   Schultz, op. cit.

7   Benioff, op. cit.

8   Steve Jobs, 2005 Stanford commencement address, YouTube, 2017.

9   Boas Shamir and Galit Eilam, "What's Your Story? A Life-Stories Approach to Authentic Leadership Development," The Leadership Quarterly, 16 (3), June 2005, pp. 395-417.

10   Shamir and Eilam, op. cit.

INDEX

Morgan James
Speakers Group

www.TheMorganJamesSpeakersGroup.com

We connect Morgan James published
authors with live and online events
and audiences who will benefit
from their expertise.

 Morgan James makes all of our titles available
through the Library for All Charity Organization.

www.LibraryForAll.org

CPSIA information can be obtained
at www.ICGtesting.com
Printed in the USA
LVOW03s0500230218
567492LV00007B/10/P